Praise for
We Have So Much In Common

We Have So Much in Common is more than a story—it's a homecoming.

Through Erin's courageous honesty and captivating storytelling, we're reminded that joy isn't something we find after healing; it's the light that leads us there. Her journey from shame to self-acceptance, from pressure to play, reveals what becomes possible when we stop striving to be enough and start remembering that we already are.

This memoir is an invitation to reconnect with your own joy—to see the beauty in your story, to laugh, to breathe, and to love yourself just as you are. Erin isn't just writing about rediscovering joy—she's living it. And through her courage, she gives us permission to do the same.

Andrea Parker, Keynote Speaker, Human Potential Expert

Erin has written the kind of book that is raw, vulnerable, and deeply human. *We Have So Much In Common* is filled with insights and perspective in this first responder world that we rarely get a glimpse into. Most importantly, Erin reminds us that shame loses its grip when we tell the truth, and that healing doesn't happen alone. Her story is a gift to anyone who's ever carried the heavy burden of trauma in silence, and acts as a reminder that the messy, hard parts of our lives are often the places where connection and brilliance are born.

Dr. Jody Carrington

This book carries such depth that it will shock you. And you won't want to put it down until you hit the last page.

Kat Weaver, Founder of Power To Pitch, Pitch & Presentation Coach

From the very first words, Erin's story gripped me and never let go. I loved her vulnerability and her book left me with the feeling that your past is never permanent, and that healing is always possible. Amazing story of overcoming pain and shame, and cultivating peace in our lives.

Kwesi Millington, Former Police Officer, Keynote Speaker & Coach

Erin Gorrie has given us a gift. A gift for all women to know they are not alone. She writes with vulnerability and truth, allowing the reader to reflect on their own circumstances and realize the core theme is the same. It is a story of perseverance and the search for self. It inspires hope, reminding us that we can all conquer our worst fears if we love ourselves first.

Krista Sherry

From the beginning Erin's book captivated me. I felt myself reflected in her words, the title resonates with the truth in all of us. I found *We Have So Much In Common* honest and relatable, every emotion coursed through me as I read Erin's story. I would recommend this book to anyone simply because we have all struggled with our sense of who we are and who the world thinks we should be.

Veronica Matthews, Owner/Breeder of Rover Barbets

Erin Gorrie bravely invites us into her story with a level of honesty and courage that is nothing short of inspiring. Her writing makes you feel as though you are standing right beside her, experiencing both the weight of her struggles and the brilliance of her resilience. Through raw and powerful life moments, she weaves together a stunning tapestry of acceptance, self-compassion, love, and joy. This book is not only a testament to her strength but also a gift to anyone seeking hope, healing, and connection. Simply brilliant!

Kimberley Cheeseman

Erin's resilience and courage are extraordinary. She's taken some of life's hardest experiences and transformed them into a story that uplifts and empowers others. It's inspiring to see her share her voice with the world.

Brendan Kane, Bestselling Author of *One Million Followers* and *Hook Point*

Erin bravely shares her painful past for all the world to see. I have no doubt that there will be some aspects of her story that will sharply resonate with every person who reads this book. In our trauma treatment program we say, "You did not go through all this for nothing.... and, Your story is not over yet." Erin has truly demonstrated that there is meaning in one's suffering and that true healing is not only possible, but it can lead to some beautiful new chapters.

Manuela Joannou M.D., Medical Director, Project Trauma Support

Erin shares her story with such vulnerability and honesty that I found myself getting chills over and over again. She speaks life into the female experience. The injustices—both big and small, that she, and women everywhere have just swallowed and accepted, no longer have power. Those experiences no longer define who she is, which gives women everywhere the permission to shed the secrecy and step into their true selves. From the moment I picked up her book, all of my responsibilities melted away. I couldn't put it down!

Jennifer Currier, Founder & Creative Director, Soirée L.A.

This book is so beautifully written. I applaud Erin's courage to dive deep, to take the time to reflect, get curious, and to seek assistance to create change. Through reading We Have So Much In Common, I reflected on my own grief, questions of why/how, and the importance of joy in our lives.

Teresa Walker, Professional Keynote Speaker and Workshop Facilitator, Kolbe Certified Consultant

Erin's choice to share her journey is a revelation for those needing to look inward and needing to understand their own path to healing. With years of recovery, and the discovery of my own people pleasing nature, Erin's stories resonated. The complete honesty and openness touched a part of me I didn't know I needed to examine. It is never too late to find your joy and reach for your dreams.

Lynn Neale

We Have So Much in Common will start to break your heart, but Erin Gorrie's brilliant writing, bravery, and honesty put it back together again, overflowing with love and stronger than ever. This is an important and beautiful memoir—I loved every page of it.

Patricia B McConnell, author of *The Education of Will* and *The Other End of the Leash*

A raw and powerful reclaiming of voice and identity, this book is an empowering call to rise above shame, adversity, and unimaginable loss. Erin redefines what it means to be enough, offering a pathway from silent suffering to speaking one's truth and transforming pain into healing, resilience, and hope.

Sarah McAlpine, RSW, Social Worker, Psychotherapist

Erin's words are a lighthouse, raw, real, and soul-stirring. She invites us to face what we've avoided, to witness our own truth, and to remember that healing isn't about fixing, it's about returning to ourselves. This book is both a comfort and a catalyst, guiding every woman back to her enoughness. A brilliantly written piece that made me feel seen alongside her

Carrie Scollon, Founder of FoundHer Retreats & Book Series

Raw, honest, and deeply personal, it felt like reading Erin's own diary. This book shines a light on how policing can consume your life and reminds us that trauma has many faces. Erin's courage in sharing her story and confronting the dangers of compartmentalization is truly inspiring.

Jen Bell

We Have So Much In Common

A Memoir

Written by Erin Gorrie

Soul Spark Publishing™

An imprint of Soul Spark Enterprises

soulsparkpublishing.com

We Have So Much In Common, First edition 2025

ISBN 978-1-964445-22-9 (paperback) 978-1-964445-23-6 (eBook)

Book Cover and Interior Formatting and Styling by Lucie Ward

We Have
So Much In
Common

Soul Spark
—PUBLISHING—

DEDICATION

For Owen and Oscar, my greatest joy and my reason for finding it again.

For Mom and Robyn, whose love I still feel beside me, guiding me always.

And for those who carry invisible injuries, who wake each day fighting battles no one can see—may you find the courage to speak your truth, the tenderness to rest, and the joy that brings you home to yourself.

CONTENTS

A NOTE FROM ERIN

This is a memoir about a full life—with all the beauty, heartbreak, complexity, and healing that can come with it.

In these pages, I share personal stories that include themes of grief, PTSD, abortion, infidelity, harassment, as well as references to multiple sclerosis (MS) and MAiD (Medical Assistance in Dying). These experiences are written from a place of tenderness and healing.

Please take care of yourself as you read. However you choose to move through these pages is the right way.

I'm so honored to share my story with you.

— Erin

PREFACE

"I want you to think about the worst trauma that you've had." The doctor's voice is calm, almost soothing, but the words land like a sledgehammer. "The moment in your life that changed you. We're going to talk about it."

I shift in my chair, the soft padding doing little to settle the weight pressing into my chest. The room is warm, welcoming, but the energy is still, almost cautious. There's a quiet apprehension in the air, a shared reservation among us, as if we're all waiting to see what this space will ask of us.

We are here for a week-long retreat for first responders and military living with PTSD—people who have spent years in survival mode, holding stories deep within ourselves that no one else could carry.

We sit in an oval, each of us in a comfortable chair, some with the ability to spin, others still. We each have a small side table, a place to set our water, our tissues,— our armor. The gas fireplace flickers beside me, casting a soft golden glow, its heat wrapping around me like a false sense of protection. I chose my chair near it intentionally. It felt safe.

Before we arrived, we were told to bring anything that would bring us comfort. A blanket, a sweater, something familiar to ground us in the discomfort we'd inevitably face. My blanket is folded neatly over my lap, as if it could somehow shield me from what's coming.

I steal a glance at the other women, some, like me, shifting in their seats, some already welling with tears. The first woman begins to speak.

And I stop breathing.

Her voice wavers as she shares. Then another woman speaks. And another. One by one, stories begin to spill out, until the room is thick with pain, old wounds rising to the surface, exposed under the soft flickering light of the fireplace.

I should be listening. I should be present for them the way they will be expected to be for me. But I can't. Because my mind is screaming at me: There is *no way* I'm saying *it*.

I force myself to breathe. To think. To find something else to talk about. The crashes. The bodies. The screams. The nightmares that used to wake me up in the middle of the night, drenched in sweat. Any one of those would be worthy of this moment. Any one of those would be acceptable.

But I know. I already know. It's not the job that needs to be heard. It's her. The girl I was at seventeen, still wide-eyed, still soft in places the world hadn't hardened yet. I was deciding for myself, tasting the freedom I had been craving, doing what I wanted simply because I could. Even if it wasn't a choice most would make. I wanted to be there. I wanted to feel grown.

That night, freedom and choices for me meant a tiny bikini, the kind that left little to the imagination. Lipstick perfect, hair just so, music pulsing in my ears. I believed I was in control of the night. And I loved it.

And then, in a moment that split my life in two, I turned and found myself face-to-face with him. My father.

His piercing blue eyes locked on mine, steady, unblinking. Not rage, not shock, something sharper. And in that instant, a wash of shame flooded me, so sudden and consuming it felt like it might drown me.

That was the night my shame was born.

I didn't know then how deeply it would take root. I didn't know it would shape my choices, my relationships, my very sense of self. But sitting here now, writing these words, I can trace so much of my life back to that one look, that one moment that told me I wasn't enough.

It also told me something worse, that I was ruined. A disappointment. What I had done was so shameful, and the judgment of others became my biggest fear. So I buried it, told no one, carrying the constant terror that one day someone would find out and expose me.

For years, I lived as though I were still that seventeen year old girl, frozen in that moment, convinced I wasn't worthy of the job, the relationship, or the life I was building. That single look branded me with shame so deep that it dictated who I believed I was, and who I believed I wasn't.

I have never spoken it. Never acknowledged it as trauma. Never even allowed myself to see it as the moment that changed everything. But it did. And that realization alone makes me feel like I might throw up. The silence around that night has lived within me for over 30 years.

Before it's my turn, we take a break. One of the male mentors stands at the edge of the room, sipping water, and I find myself moving toward him before I even realize what I'm doing.

"Can I ask you something?"

He looks at me, really looks at me, and suddenly I feel seen in a way that makes my throat tighten.

"You have something, don't you?" he says.

A lump forms instantly. He knows.

I swallow. Hard. My hands are sweaty, my stomach knots.

"I....I don't know. Maybe."

He nods like he understands exactly where I am right now.

"I have two questions for you," he said. "If not now, when? And, if not here, where?"

His words send a shockwave through me. I hate that they make sense. I hate that I already know the answer. But saying it? Speaking the words out loud? No. Absolutely not.

We return to the circle. The woman next to me begins speaking, sharing her story with an openness that guts me. She is brave. She does not hold back. And I feel like a coward.

And then, it's my turn.

The lump in my throat swells. My stomach churns. My hands tremble. And then, I start to talk.

My body screams at me to stop. My brain begs me to find another way out. But the words spill anyway.

"My worst trauma happened when I was seventeen."

The room goes silent. I keep going.

"I lived in a small town, about an hour and a half east of the city. After a breakup, I was feeling lost, and my aunt and uncle, who I adored, offered me the chance to spend the summer with them, babysitting my cousins. They had a pool. They were fun. It was an escape. I said yes without hesitation."

I shift in my chair unable to get comfortable, my fingers gripping the fabric of my blanket. The warmth from the fireplace suddenly feels suffocating.

"While I was there, I had a friend, a girl a year older than me who was working as a nanny in a nearby town. One night, while flipping through a magazine, we came across an ad for a bar. Exotic Dancers wanted. I didn't understand what it was at first. 'What's an exotic dancer, I asked?' 'A stripper, you dummy!' I laughed. But when I looked at her again, her expression had changed. She wasn't joking."

"So I told her honestly what was racing through my head: Could we actually do this? Could we really walk into a bar like that? Could we step onto a stage in barely anything at all? Could we stand under those lights, exposed, next to women who were older, more beautiful, more experienced than us?"

"She looked me right in the eyes and said, hell ya we can"

My voice cracks.

"I remembered my ex-boyfriend saying I could easily work at a place like that. And for whatever reason, those words lodged themselves in my brain. So that Friday night, we went. We walked in, met the owner, and with barely a glance, he waved us in. No ID check. Nothing. We looked the part, and that was all that mattered."

My hands are shaking as I'm telling the room this story. I can feel their eyes on me.

"That became my evening job for the rest of the summer. And then, when summer ended, I kept going back. Weekends, whenever I could. I loved the freedom. The thrill. I didn't see the danger. I didn't understand it yet."

I swallow hard. The next part is the worst part of the story.

"One night, close to closing time, I had just finished a private dance. Back then, you stood on a small box in front of the customer, no contact. I turned around and..."

My breath catches trying to finish.

"...I was face-to-face with my father."

Silence. I don't dare look up.

"The terror that shot through me in that moment, it's still in me. My brain froze. And then, after what felt like an eternity but was probably just seconds, I blurted out, 'What are you doing here?'"

"And he said, 'What are YOU doing here?'"

I shift some more in my seat, when did this chair become so uncomfortable??, *rubbing my sweaty palms on my thighs, my voice thick with emotion, barely able to continue.*

"I ran. I ran all the way upstairs to the dressing room. The other girls helped me gather my things, asking me what was wrong. And then I heard him, my dad's voice booming from downstairs. He was demanding answers from the owner. Yelling at him. Telling him I was underage. Telling him he was a cop."

Tears well in my eyes. I don't try to stop them.

"One of the girls snuck me out the back. My boyfriend was waiting in the car, engine running. I jumped in, and we drove. I spent the night at his house, terrified my dad would follow. Something in me knew—I could never go home again.

I pause, the weight of the memories crushing me.

I wipe my eyes.

"From that moment forward, I buried it. I told no one. Only a handful of people in my life ever knew. But I carried it, terrified that someone at work would find out. That my past would be used against me. That I would never be seen as good enough."

I stop. It's all out now. It finally exists outside of me. I finally raise my eyes.

The doctor looks at me, her face filled with sadness.

"Erin, you are not that seventeen year old girl. You've been carrying her shame for thirty years, but you are not her anymore."

Her words broke something open in me. For so long, I had held onto that shame like it was a part of my body, gripping it so tightly I didn't even realize how much it weighed me down. But with her words, she gave me permission to set it down.

She heard every word I said, and yet she didn't look at me the way my dad had that night. She didn't judge me. She didn't recoil. Instead, she met my eyes with a kind of steady presence that felt almost foreign, like she could hold my story without trying to fix it or make it smaller.

For the first time, someone allowed me to see that night as exactly what it was, a single moment. Not a definition. Not a scarlet letter I had to carry forever. A decision that, sure, some would call reckless. But to me, it was a choice I made for myself, on my own terms, because I wanted to, and that mattered.

No one had ever told me that before. No one had ever said that at forty-six, I didn't have to keep identifying as that ashamed seventeen year old girl. And as I sat there, I couldn't help but think, *If she, someone wise and insightful, doesn't find me disgraceful, then why do I?*

It wasn't just her kindness. It was the way her words slipped past my defenses and landed somewhere deeper. They loosened something I had kept sealed for years. And in that space, I saw it, this wasn't a life sentence. It wasn't who I was anymore. And after being wound tightly around every part of my being, the shame began to loosen its grip.

That moment didn't fix everything. It wasn't magic. The shame wasn't wiped clean. But it was the beginning. A beginning. I had spoken my truth, and the world didn't fall apart. The women in that room held me with their understanding, their silence, their compassion.

In a way I never had before, I let myself believe that maybe I could heal. Maybe I could let it go.

I woke up early every morning at that retreat, lacing up my runners before most people were out of bed. The gym was quiet at that hour, just the hum of the treadmill and the steady rhythm of my footsteps. It was the only part of my day that still felt familiar. The rest of it, the group sessions, the uncomfortable self-reflection, the peeling back of layers I had spent decades protecting, felt completely foreign.

I wasn't strong during that time of my life. Not physically, not emotionally. I ate healthy because I knew I should, not because I had an appetite. I was exhausted, drained in a way that went beyond just needing sleep. This retreat was supposed to help, but all it seemed to be doing was pulling me into thoughts I had worked so hard to avoid. But maybe the retreat wasn't here to comfort me, it was here to confront me.

The room where we gathered each day was warm, comfortable, designed to make us feel safe. But safety is a strange thing when you're being asked to look at parts of yourself you've never dared to examine. That next morning, I took my usual seat near the fireplace, wrapping my hands around my coffee, letting its familiar warmth try to ground me, offering me a modicum of solace.

The doctor stood at the front of the room, calm and steady, speaking as if she already knew that what she was about to say would shake us.

"You create the life you live."

I had heard it before, but this time, I really listened.

"You attract the people in your life. If you look closely, you'll see the patterns. The relationships you find yourself in, your friendships, your partners, it's often a mirror of what you knew in childhood. Not because it's right, not because it's healthy, but because it's familiar."

I stared down at my hands, heat creeping up my neck.

"If you grew up in a household with a controlling parent—maybe a father who struggled to regulate his emotions, who yelled, who needed to control the family dynamic—you may find yourself in a relationship with someone just like that. Even if you swore you never would. Because love, to your subconscious, looks like what you've always known."

A rush of understanding hit me hard. My heart pounded in my chest, but I kept my face neutral. I had vowed never to be with someone like my father. Never. I hated how he would blow up, how rigid his thinking was, how everything was black and white, how it always felt like he was in charge and my mother just followed along. I had spent my entire life rejecting that dynamic.

And yet, here I was.

My partner was the same. The same inflexibility, the same unshakable certainty that his way was the only way. Even the teasing, the relentless poking, the "just joking," the "lighten up" comments that always left me feeling like there was some truth buried underneath the humor, it was all the same.

Even my friendships. I was always the easy one. The neutral one. Switzerland. The friend who never had an opinion on where we ate, what we did, who let others take the lead. I never wanted to make waves. I never wanted to be the difficult one.

Had I done this? Had I unknowingly built a life filled with people who mirrored the very things I swore I would never repeat?

I sat with that thought all day. Even after the session ended, even after I returned to my small retreat room, a basic space with a single bed, a sink, and a nightstand. It wouldn't leave me.

Had I really created this life? My life? For comfort? For familiarity? Had I chosen to struggle because it felt normal?

I curled up on the bed, staring at the ceiling, exhausted by my own thoughts.

Later in the week, the doctor spoke again, this time about something I had never heard of: Occupational Stress Injury.

"It's not just the trauma itself that breaks people down," she said. "It's the betrayal. The isolation. The way the very systems meant to protect you, fail you."

I felt my chest tighten.

She talked about sanctuary trauma, a term I had never come across before. It was the betrayal, the injustice, the anger that comes from being abandoned by the very people and systems you believed would protect you.

It was like she was reading my mind.

My police service didn't care about me. No one called just to check in, to see if I was okay. The only contact I got was from people who wanted to know if and when I was coming back. That was it. Nine years in the job, and the second I wasn't useful, I was discarded.

And yet, here was this doctor, standing in front of me, telling me that this wasn't some personal failing. That the anger, the hurt, the complete sense of betrayal I carried wasn't just mine, it was real. It had a name. Sanctuary trauma.

She described moral injury—not just witnessing horrific things, but being forced to participate in them. Doing things you never wanted to do. Saying things you never wanted to say. The kind of wounds that don't heal because they aren't just physical, they're soul-deep.

"Moral injuries," she said, "are often the ones that drive people to suicide. Because they attack your sense of who you are."

I swallowed hard.

And then she said something else, something that unraveled me completely.

"PTSD is an injury. Not a disorder. It's not something wrong with you. It's something that happened to you."

I had spent months feeling like something was wrong with me. That I was broken. That I had failed. But as I listened, learning for the first time that PTSD wasn't a disorder but an injury, something shifted. Injuries heal. Not always quickly. Not always completely. But with time, there can be healing. And so I considered that maybe I could heal too. Maybe I wouldn't ever be the same, but maybe that wasn't a bad thing.

I had spent the last number of months trying to heal alone. Trying to figure it out by myself. But she stressed the importance of community, of connection, that you cannot heal from this alone.

And then she said something else that wouldn't leave me.

"The people who find a way through this are the ones who find meaning in their story."

I sat there, staring at her, stuck on those words.

Find meaning in my story? In all of this? How? I was broken. I had been discarded. I had nothing. How could I possibly turn that into something good? But the way she said it, it wasn't just wishful thinking. It was truth.

She talked about how the happiest people in life have something they love, something that pulls them into joy, a hobby, a passion, a way to step outside of themselves.

And I had nothing.

For years, my job had been my joy. It had been my identity, my everything. I worked, I raised my kids, and that was it. There was no hobby. No passion. No outlet. Just work and survival.

And now, without the job, what was left?

I didn't know.

But, I started to wonder if maybe, just maybe, there could be something... something else, something more.

Turns out, this book is the something that grew out of all of it, the grief, the silence, the survival.

CLEAN SLATE

The wheels of the plane touched the tarmac with a jolt, and I opened my eyes to find California waiting for me. It was October 1994, I was nineteen years old, wide-eyed, exhausted, and utterly convinced that Los Angeles was about to change everything.

I turned toward the window, resting my forehead on the cold plastic frame. The clouds had cleared somewhere over the desert, and now everywhere I looked the view was golden. Sunlight bounced off rooftops and billboards. Palm trees lined the roads like sentinels. And the sky, that sky was unlike anything I'd seen before. Endless. Open. It felt like permission to live life the same way—endlessly, openly, vividly. Even inside the plane's cabin, I could feel the heat. It wasn't just temperature, it was energy. Like the city had its own pulse, and I was about to step into the rhythm.

As we taxied on the runway, the sun streamed through the window and warmed my face. I closed my eyes and let it sink deep into me. I wanted to hold onto it, to bottle this exact sensation—the quiet certainty that something was beginning. It had been years since my chest felt this open, my mind this unguarded.

I felt completely suspended in hope, untethered from the girl I had been, not yet knowing the woman I would become, but sure that this place, this moment, this bridge between the past and the future, would change me.

We exited the plane directly onto the tarmac, stairs down to the pavement, like in an old movie. It made it feel like an arrival, not just a landing. And the second I stepped outside, it hit me. The smell.

It's hard to explain unless you've been there. Dry and warm, with just a hint of salt and sun and something sweet, like possibility laced with gasoline. Even now, when I return, it's the first thing I notice. A smell that means possibility, escape, and becoming.

That day, it smelled like everything behind me was staying behind me. The fresh air was a fresh start. The sweet smell was a sweet new beginning.

My boyfriend and I had come here chasing exactly that—a fresh start, a chance to follow our dreams in a city where it seemed anything could happen.

We walked toward the parking area, squinting in the sunlight, dragging our suitcases like anchors. My boyfriend's friend, a wild, flamboyant music promoter pulled up in his white convertible muscle car that looked like it belonged in a scene from *Entourage*. Of course he did. This was Los Angeles. Everything was a performance.

We tossed our bags in the back, climbed in, and sped north on the freeway, wind in our hair, sun on our faces, and a kind of reckless optimism in my chest that felt almost childlike. I wasn't afraid. Not even a little. And looking back, that shocks me.

I had no plan. No job. No contacts. But I wasn't scared because he was with me. He always made me feel safe. Like whatever happened, we'd figure it out together. As long as he was by my side, I could breathe.

And maybe that's why I didn't look back. This was my clean slate.

No one here knew my past. No one would whisper. No one would judge. No one would look at me and think: I know what she did. The girl I was, the girl who had made choices to survive, to feel powerful, to be seen, she was staying behind. I could finally become someone else. Anyone else. In L.A., you can be anyone you want. And who I wanted to be wasn't anything like the girl I was leaving behind.

The room was dimly lit, barely cutting through the haze of cigarette smoke. A woman moved across the stage with effortless confidence, her body swaying to the slow, hypnotic beat. She was captivating. To my seventeen year old self, this was glamor—bold, powerful women, mysterious shadows, and a room charged with something electric. It was unlike anything I had ever seen, and everything about it pulled me in. When the door to that world opened, I didn't hesitate. I stepped right through.

It started with a newspaper ad my girlfriend and I saw—exotic dancers wanted, an offer to make money, fast. It seemed simple enough, just dancing. But the moment I walked through those bar doors, I entered another universe. The pounding bass echoed in my chest, lights flashing through the smoke like beacons. The air was thick with whispers and want. I had never felt so far from home. The whole scene excited me.

The owner barely looked at us before barking, "Go change into bikinis." No questions. No IDs. Just a glance and he decided I was good enough. I learned that night that my value wasn't in who I was, or what I could do. it was in how I looked. That was enough for him.

When we first arrived, they told us we needed stage names. Something exotic. Something mysterious. I was already struggling to figure out who I was, who "Erin" was. Now I had to create someone new. It felt like both an opportunity and a betrayal. But the persona became a mask, and I wore it well.

The first time I stepped onto that stage, I felt the weight of every gaze settle on me. Most of the men were older, their eyes locked on me with an intensity I had never experienced. For a girl who had always craved attention, it felt intoxicating. Suddenly, I wasn't invisible. I was wanted. Admired. Their gaze touched a hollow space inside me I hadn't known existed. I learned quickly. Learned what to say, how to move, how to read a room. I gave them what they wanted, a fantasy, a story made up on the spot. And in return, I got what I thought I needed, validation. It was a dangerous, seductive game. But with each night, I slipped further away from who I really was. In their eyes, I could be anything. And somewhere along the way, I forgot how to just be me.

That single moment, staring into my father's eyes, split my life in two. It wasn't one of those moments when you look back and see that it was defining. I knew it immediately. There was a before path, and now everything else was on the after path. There would be no going back.

The car we were driving, the one my dad had given me, suddenly felt like a trap. I was sure he'd report it stolen. I was sure he'd come for it. It wasn't just a car anymore. It was everything that had just come crashing down.

My dad had always told me, "You can be anything, but don't be a liar. I hate liars." And I had lied. Over and over. I had hidden a life from him, and now it was exposed. The trust was gone. I couldn't live at home anymore. If I stayed, I'd be under lock and key. The taste of freedom I had just discovered would be nothing more than a memory.

The next morning, I called home. When my dad answered, I said, "Hi."

Silence.

Then my mom was on the line. Her voice was different, not angry, just wounded. She asked if I was okay. I told her I was bringing the car back. That I was moving out. She told me I didn't have to. But I knew I did.

Later that day, I returned the car. Packed my things. My mom cried. My sister cried. My dad? He didn't look at me. The only words he said were, "If you ever go back to one of those bars, I'll drag you out myself." That was it. The only time he ever acknowledged what happened. We never talked about it again. Not once.

But I lived with it.

I carried the shame of that night for decades. I lived as that seventeen year old girl, paralyzed by his eyes, by his silence, by that one line. I let it shape how I saw myself, what I thought I deserved.

And it wasn't just my parents I left that night.

I left my sister.

The one who had been by my side from the beginning. The one who shared my secrets, my bedroom, my world. I didn't think about what it meant for her when I left. I didn't realize the whispers would find her too. That she'd be left to defend me, alone, while people judged and speculated.

I abandoned her without realizing it. And it's something that fed my shame long after the experience passed. I didn't just walk away from my family that night and the life I had known, I left behind pieces of myself I wouldn't find again for years.

From that day forward, my relationship with my dad was never the same. Months passed before he truly spoke to me again. The silence became its own language, a heavy, unspoken truth that hovered in the air.

I moved in with my boyfriend to take some time to figure things out. After hearing my fathers words, "If you end up in one of those bars again, I'll come drag you out myself." I was terrified. So I didn't go back.

Instead, I started looking for modeling work, clinging to the dream I'd carried for years. Runways, photo shoots, glossy magazines, that was the world I imagined for myself, the one that felt safe and familiar, where the lights were bright but the attention wasn't dangerous. In that world, I could perform, transform, and play a role without feeling like I was being devoured.

That's when I came across a listing for a lingerie boutique hiring live models. It sounded perfect. Walk the runway and showcase outfits for men shopping for their wives.

Later that day I walked into the boutique, a dimly lit store filled with racks of lace and silk, and was greeted by the owner, a short, older woman with an accent so thick I had to lean in to catch her words. She gave me a quick tour of the front of the store, then led me to the back where things began to not quite match up with my expectations.

Behind a discreet door were a series of private rooms, each with a short runway and a single chair at the end. Off to the side, a changing screen stood in each room. She explained the process, the customer would choose the lingerie, and I would model it for him, alone, in that room.

"There are cameras in every room," she said, waving her hand casually. "For safety."

I paused, internally but I didn't ask questions.

I told myself it was just modeling. But the truth is, I didn't feel confident. I felt unsure. A little dizzy. Like I'd stepped into something I wasn't quite prepared for. Something felt off.

But I needed the work. I needed to prove that I could survive on my own. That I could land on my feet, even if I was still figuring out who I was. So I smiled. Nodded. Agreed to come back the next day.

I'll never forget my first customer.

He was older, polished, and businesslike. The kind of man who might have passed me on the street and nodded politely. The kind of man I'd been told would be shopping for his wife.

I slipped into a red lace number, barely a slip and stepped out onto the short runway. As I walked toward him, he smiled and nodded, like we were in on some strange, silent agreement. At the end of the runway, I turned to walk back, keeping my movements slow, just like I'd been taught.

But when I turned again at the top and looked back down at him, his pants were unzipped. He was touching himself. I froze for a moment, unsure of what to do. I didn't say a word. I didn't dare make eye contact, I just kept walking up and down. After what felt like an eternity, he was done. He thanked me, dropped cash into a little clear box, cleared his throat, and said, "You are stunning," before turning and walking out. I stood there, unsure of how to feel. I was in shock, but I didn't have the luxury of falling apart. I had more appointments that day, more booked for the week.

So I told myself it was fine.
That this was normal.
That I was in control.

But beneath the surface, it didn't feel right. I was already starting to disconnect from myself, rationalizing, numbing, making it through each hour just to make it through the day.

And I went back the next day. Then the next. And the next.

More men. More cash.

But something inside me was starting to split. My body kept showing up, going through the motions, but my mind began drifting somewhere far away, somewhere I didn't have to feel the confusion, the shame, the strange ache I couldn't name.

I kept going for weeks. A month, maybe more.
But by the end, I knew I couldn't do it anymore.

It wasn't about being too soft, or too sensitive, or not strong enough. It was about the silence in my body. The numbness. How quickly I learned to shut down just to stay standing.

I left and never went back.

And I told no one.

I didn't talk about it. Not to friends. Not to family. Not even to myself.

I folded the memory up like a worn piece of paper and tucked it somewhere deep, somewhere dark. The creases are as fresh as the day I folded it. I don't ever take it out to look at. It didn't feel like trauma. It felt like something I should've expected. Something I should've known better about.

That's what shame does. It doesn't scream. It whispers: You should've known. You brought this on yourself. Just forget about it. Don't make it a big deal.

So I didn't.

I moved on, at least on the outside. But something in me went quiet. The trust I had in people, especially men, grew dimmer. And the trust I had in myself? It began to fray.

I started believing my body was only valuable if someone else wanted it. That *I* was only valuable when my body was wanted. That I was safest when I didn't make a fuss. That my silence was a kind of power, even though it was really just fear in disguise.

I didn't understand then how experiences like that linger. How they burrow beneath your skin and become the lens you see yourself through.

And instead of letting in the light of who I really was, my worth, my voice, my truth. I tried to cover it up.

With busyness. With performance. With perfection.

With survival.

Eventually, my dad offered to help pay for my apartment if I went back to school. So I tried. I lasted three days. I didn't belong there. Not in a classroom. Not at a desk. I wasn't a teenager anymore. I had seen too much. I needed to survive. And the only thing I knew how to do was dance.

So I did. Quietly. Carefully. Moving from bar to bar. Always scared my father might walk through the door again. But I played the role. Told him I was in school. Kept the lie alive. Until I met someone who offered me a way out.

He believed in me. He wanted a future with me. That made me believe in myself, just enough to try again.

We made a plan: save money, finish school, move to L.A. A fresh start. A clean slate.

So I did what I had to do. I finished high school. I went to every modeling audition I could. Fashion shows, commercial castings, photo shoots, saying yes to anything that offered even a glimmer of possibility.

And at night, I danced.

Not for attention. Not for fun. But for freedom. Every tip, every song, every late night was a step closer to that ticket out.

I told myself it was fine because it wouldn't be forever. Just a few more months. Just until we moved to LA. I clung to that timeline like it could save me.

And when that plane landed on October 31, 1994…

I felt like I was flying toward a version of myself I hadn't met yet.

The girl who survived was on that plane.

But the woman stepping onto the tarmac, was who I was becoming. She was going to rewrite her story, leave it all beyond, and start fresh. I didn't look back. I was done. Los Angeles was my reset.

I got a job in a coffee shop not long after we arrived in L.A. It was tucked into a little neighborhood, full of regulars and tourists, creative types and dreamers, people with sunglasses and notebooks, screenplays in their bags and headphones on their ears. I wore an apron. I smiled. I learned how to remember faces. And I spoke with the kind of practiced charm that made people feel seen, without ever letting them see me. And I loved it.

There was something quietly redemptive about making lattes in Los Angeles—just for a time.
Behind that counter, I wasn't the girl from the club, the dancer, the one that left her home, her mother, her sister, herself. The one who disappointed her father. I was just a girl in a coffee shop. Starting over.

No one looked at me like I was broken. No one expected an explanation. I felt safe in the anonymity, in the stillness, in the freedom of being unseen. I had tried for so many years to be seen, but here, being just the anonymous girl making the latte, I could breathe. She was still inside me, the girl I had been. But here, I could let her rest.

NAKED

I t was the middle of the night when my phone lit up. The room was silent, still, except for the white noise of the baseboard heater and the soft breaths of my boys asleep in the next room. My body stirred before my mind could catch up, already half-braced for something urgent. The screen glowed beside me. A single vibration. One message.

I had started keeping the ringer on my cell phone in case work needed me. So even in my sleep, I was half-listening. Always. I reached for the phone, bleary-eyed, heart beginning to stir. And then I read it,

Did you know your Playboy video is on Amazon now? It's being sold on DVD. Thought you'd like to know.

The words didn't land all at once. They bled in slowly, letter by letter like a typewriter inking a page, until my breath caught and heat flashed through my body like I'd touched something electric.

I sat up too fast. The air felt thin. Stomach churning. Skin cold. That sick, sinking feeling that something I'd left behind was about to surface in a world that wouldn't understand, and might not forgive.

The name on the screen confirmed what my body already knew. Only one person could send something like that, not to inform, but to remind me he still could.

I stared at the message, and a wave of fear crashed over me. No, not just fear. Terror.

I had worked so hard for this life. I had sacrificed, studied, clawed my way through training, all to give my boys something steady, something safe. Becoming a police officer wasn't just a job. It was a promise, to them, and to myself. And now it felt threatened.

And he was threatening all of it. Why? Was it control? Spite? A reminder that no matter how far I had come, no matter how I'd woven a new life so far from what was, he still had a hand on the thread?

Whatever it was, it worked. That sick, sinking feeling took hold, the helplessness of knowing someone could unravel everything you'd built with a single story.

What would happen if he told? If he said it out loud? If he exposed the version of me I had tried so hard to bury?

I had moved on. I wasn't that girl anymore, the one that would do anything to be noticed. But there, in my bed in the early hours of the morning, the memories came flooding back.

The studio was tucked into one of those strange industrial corridors L.A. is full of—beige doors, buzzing fluorescent lights, and a pervasive cloud of secrecy. The producer's name was printed neatly on the door, as if that made everything inside official. But it still felt off. Like something was being hidden in plain sight.

Inside, a few women sat, flipping through fashion magazines on the coffee table. It wasn't like the TV or commercial auditions I'd gone to before, where people chatted nervously or rehearsed lines from scripts. Here, there were no words to break the tension. Just the soft click of heels crossing and uncrossing. We were all dressed the same, tight little mini dresses, sky-high heels, makeup done to perfection. Ready. Polished. Masks and body armor on.

But under all of it, we were quiet. Still. Each of us pretending to be relaxed, but bracing in our own way. Measuring each other. Wondering what exactly we were waiting for, and what we were willing to trade for the chance to be chosen.

I'd been in a place like this before, just a few weeks earlier at the Playboy head office, testing for the spot of Playmate. That space had a similar feel, beige walls, humming fluorescents, but the energy couldn't have been more different. The Playboy offices were crowded and alive, full of chatter, movement and nerves disguised as confidence. Women compared outfits, practiced poses and filled the air with small talk as they waited their turn on the carousel of possibility.

This place was the opposite. The silence was unnerving. And the opportunity was different, too. I wasn't here for the centerfold track. This was another branch of the Playboy empire—their video division and the man I was about to meet had been producing for them for years.

My name was called, and I stood, instinctively tugging my dress down as I followed a tall, beautiful woman through the hallway. She moved like she belonged there, confident, composed, unreadable. She led me into a quiet office where an older man with a trimmed beard and wire-framed glasses sat behind a desk. He looked up and offered a soft, practiced smile. She introduced him as the producer of the video.

He stood as I entered, reaching out to shake my hand. "Wow," he said, his eyes scanning me. "You are beautiful. Lovely smile."

He explained that he had worked with Playboy for years, producing videos for their different series. But this one, he said, was different.

This project is about real women, he told me. Natural. Not enhanced. "That's what we're celebrating here: beauty without surgery. Authenticity."

He used words like "natural" and "authentic" as if they meant something new, something rare. And right then I wanted to believe they did. I wanted to believe I was being chosen for something meaningful. That there was value in showing up just as I was. In a world full of polished perfection, I was being cast as the exception. And I wasn't sure if that made me special, or simply marketable in a different way.

After he finished explaining the direction of the videos, he pointed me down the hallway to a small curtained dressing space.

"There's a robe there," he said. "You can slip it on, and we'll get some Polaroids to start."

Polaroids were standard back then, a quick, raw capture to see exactly what you looked like without camera makeup, styling, or studio lighting. They knew how much transformation could happen in front of a camera. But this was about the blank canvas. The Polaroid gave them the unfiltered truth. They would use them as reference. Line them up. Decide who would be chosen based not on angles or touch-ups, but on how your natural features held up under the lens.

It wasn't glamorous. It was exposing.

I stood there in the changing space, holding the thin white robe in my hands.

There's something unspoken in moments like that, when the curtain's drawn and your body becomes a kind of transaction. I could hear the producer's voice just outside, waiting for me to be ready. There was no set. No big production. Just natural light, an open space, and the quiet pressure of being watched before you even step out.

The robe felt light, almost weightless, and yet it carried everything. The hope of being chosen. The fear of being discarded. The familiar ache of not knowing if you're enough, or too much, or about to be judged for both.

I tied it at the waist, stepped barefoot onto the cold floor, and opened the curtain.

"Just come stand right in front of this backdrop," he said.

The room was sterile in a way I hadn't expected: white backdrop, one assistant, one producer. Faint buzz of fluorescent lighting. It felt more like a medical exam.

He gestured toward me. "Whenever you're ready."

Undressing in front of someone you don't know isn't about seduction, it's about judgement. Not about connection, but about approval. It wasn't about being seen. It was about being chosen.

I remember the chill. Not just in the room, but on my skin. That brief pause when the fabric left my body and I stood there, exposed, and somehow more invisible than I'd ever been.

I posed. I turned. I smiled slightly. The camera clicked. Polaroids spit out like receipts. I did what was asked. I held my ground.

On the outside, I looked composed. Confident, even. But inside, something softened. Something quieted. Not fear exactly. But a flicker of something I didn't yet have words for.

Afterward, I sat again in the changing area, the robe crumpled in my lap. The same body. The same face. But I looked at myself differently. Was this empowerment? Was I claiming my body, or letting it be claimed?

I told myself I had control. That this was a choice. And in some ways, it was. But it also felt familiar. The way it felt to be wanted just enough to be used. The way attention masquerades as approval. The way my silence wrapped around me tighter than the robe ever had.

I walked out with the hopes they would call. And one question I didn't want to answer: Am I doing this because I want to… or because I still believe it's all I'm good for?

When I moved to L.A., I told myself I was leaving the past behind. That I was building something new. Something respectable. Something worthy.

But even there, even under the illusion of choice and confidence, I found myself accepting the same kind of attention that once defined my survival. I wasn't dancing anymore. I wasn't on stage. I wasn't modeling lingerie. But I was still saying yes to the same belief: If someone sees me, maybe I exist.

It wasn't that I had no boundaries. I had a clear line. I never crossed into pornography. I never even considered it. But what made this acceptable? Why was this the edge I was willing to walk?

Some women wouldn't have gone near Playboy. Others went much further. I lived in the middle, telling myself I was empowered, while secretly wondering if I was still just building a newer, more experienced version of the same mask.

Only days later, my phone rang. "Hi Erin," the voice said warmly. It was the producer. "My team and I looked over your photos, and we think you'd be a perfect fit for the video. We're highlighting naturally beautiful women, and you're exactly what we're looking for."

He went on to explain the dates, the plan, and told me someone from the team would be in touch to go over details.

I could barely contain my excitement. As soon as I hung up, I screamed with joy. This was big. I was going to be in a Playboy video. Not a background role. Not a maybe. They wanted me.

At the time, I didn't think about what it might mean years down the line to have a video like that out in the world. I didn't consider how it might resurface, or who might one day see it. All I could feel was how proud I was. How legitimate it felt.

Years later, those memories and emotions came rushing back, but coloured over by two decades. The pride I felt that day wasn't the same now. Now I was living the consequences. In the dark. With a single text. From someone who knew how to shake the ground beneath me with nothing more than a sentence.

"Thought you'd like to know."

It wasn't information. It wasn't a heads up. It was a threat. And I felt all of it deep in my bones.

The terror that the police would find out. That it would somehow make me unfit. Unworthy. That everything I'd worked for could be unraveled by one piece of plastic, one DVD on Amazon, one click from the wrong person.

But that fear wasn't really about the video. It was about me. It was about the version of me who said yes that day. The one I hadn't forgiven. The one I hadn't yet understood.

I see her now, the woman in that studio, holding the robe, hoping she was enough. She wasn't desperate. She was determined. She wasn't weak. She was powerful. Trying to be chosen. Trying to believe that someone could look at her and say: You're worth something.

I don't shame her anymore. I don't need to explain her, not even to myself. I just hold her, with compassion, with understanding, and with the power she didn't know she had.

That flimsy robe doesn't represent exposure anymore. It represents the moment I began to realize I could stop hiding. That I could tell the story myself, without fear of what someone else might do with it.

Because yes, the video is out there. But the difference is… I'm not afraid of being found out anymore.

I've already found myself.

And in freeing myself from the secrets I once believed were shameful, I've set myself free.

MY FAULT

I was scrolling through my phone when I saw the headline. Another high-profile sexual assault case. Another not guilty verdict. My stomach dropped, not because I was surprised, but because I wasn't.

It hit me harder than I expected. That familiar lump in my throat. That feeling of being twenty-three again. Or forty-three. Or any of the other ages I was when men did things they shouldn't have, and I said nothing.

This is why women don't speak. Because even when we do, even when we remember everything in detail—the floor, the music, the smell of beer, the heat of someone's breath, they still don't believe us.

Or worse, they do… and they just don't care.

The verdict didn't just stir up rage, it shook loose two memories I'd tucked away long ago.

They were different in every way.
Different decades.
Different jobs.
Different versions of me.

But the feeling?
The shame?
The way I made myself smaller to survive? Those parts were the same.

My then husband and I had just moved back from Los Angeles and bought a small house, trying to piece together some version of stability. Not long after, I got a job at a British pub through a friend. I had barely any bartending experience, certainly not pouring draft from a real tap.

I remember when I went in for my interview the owner asked me to reach for the glasses on the highest shelf above the bar. I didn't think much of it then, just ensuring I could actually get the glasses down myself. But my shirt lifted a bit, exposing my midriff. I caught him nodding to himself. He knew exactly what he was doing, and it wasn't making sure I could reach the glasses off the top shelf.

He knew his regulars, the same men who lined the bar each night, pints in hand, eyes roaming. He hired me for them. And I knew how to smile, tie my shirt into a crop top, and pretend not to notice.

Wednesday nights were always busy. Local sports teams would come in after their games, rowdy and hungry, ordering pitchers of beer and baskets of wings.

This Wednesday night felt like any other. Two fresh pitchers sweated in my hands as I crossed the floor toward the high-top in the corner. A group of men were crammed around it, shoulders bumping, voices raised above the music. Plates of wings and fries cluttered the table. The pub was alive with noise, pool balls cracking in the corner, glasses clinking at the bar, bursts of laughter that rose and fell like waves. I reached their table, bending slightly to set the pitchers down. And that's when I felt it.

A hand.
Up my skirt.
Flesh on flesh.
Uninvited. Unmistakable.

I froze. For half a second, the world stopped moving. The laughter blurred. The voices muted. All I could hear was my own heartbeat, pounding in my ears like an alarm.

I straightened slowly, as if moving too fast might make it more real. My breath caught. I turned, wide-eyed, scanning the group.

They were laughing.
Not nervously. Not apologetically.

They were amused. Like it was nothing.

They pointed at each other, shrugging, pretending to deflect, but not really caring who had done it. Because to them, it didn't matter. I didn't matter. To them, I was part of the game.

I didn't scream. I didn't cry. I didn't even speak. I just stepped back into myself, silently.

And then came the shame. Not theirs, mine.

Why did you bend over that way?
Why didn't you say something?
What did you expect, dressed like this?

The questions came fast and hard, and every single answer pointed back at me. That was the story I had always known. If a boundary was crossed, it was because I wasn't careful enough, that it was my fault somehow.

They left me a big tip that night. More than usual. More than I deserved for a few pitchers and a round of wings and fries. And I knew why. It wasn't generosity. It was guilt. Or maybe arrogance. As if money could smooth over what happened. As if a few extra bills on the table could make me forget the hand up my skirt.

I thought about telling my husband when I got home. I sat in the driveway for a minute too long. Practiced how I might say it. But all I could think was: What if he gets mad and makes me quit?

I didn't want to lose the job. I didn't want to deal with his reaction. So I said nothing. I told no one. I kept going to work. But I hated Wednesdays after that.

I hated walking in and seeing those same men at the same table, week after week, laughing like nothing ever happened. Their presence was a weekly reminder of my silence, of the shame that I now carried.

I found myself torn, between wanting to dress the way I always had, and not wanting to give anyone the wrong idea.

As if the way I looked gave them permission.
As if I had done something wrong.

That moment left me feeling small. Helpless. And ashamed.

Years passed. Different jobs. Different uniforms. Each time, I told myself I was stronger now. Safer somehow. But the truth is, it happened again. And again. Sometimes in ways that were easier to brush aside, the kind you try to forget before they take root.

But this time was different. By then, I was in policing. I had just finished a high-level course, passed the exam after weeks of study and stress. A group of us went to a bar to celebrate. I remember walking in that night feeling light. Proud. Not showy, but steady, like the hard work had finally earned me a seat at the table.

We weren't in uniform, but I still carried the weight of it. That invisible badge of approval. I had done something hard. I had made it through. And I wanted to belong.

The bar was dim and warm, the kind of place where the lights hang low and the conversation wraps around you. I slid into a bench seat at a long wooden table, colleagues crowding in on either side. Coats were off. Drinks in hand. Laughter came easy. It was one of those rare moments of camaraderie, when you let your guard down just enough to feel like part of something.

Then he slid in beside me. An officer I didn't know well. Drunk. Loud. Way too close. His thigh pressed against mine. His arm brushed my shoulder. I froze, waiting for him to shift. He didn't.

I looked across the table, instructors, sergeants, people I respected.
They saw it.
They noticed.

And they laughed. Laughed like it was harmless. Like this kind of thing just happened when you were blowing off steam.

I didn't laugh.
I didn't move.
I just sat there, shrinking inch by inch inside myself.

Eventually, I found an excuse. "Bathroom," I said quietly.

The only way out was past him. I didn't ask anyone to move. I didn't make a scene. I just slid sideways, trying to be small. Invisible. And that's when it happened.

A loud slap. The sting. His hand, right across my ass. Time stopped. The room went quiet. Conversations stuttered. Forks paused halfway to mouths. Everyone heard it.

I stood still, spine rigid, eyes locked on the floor. My skin burned hot. Humiliation seared through me like fire, not just from the touch, but from the silence that followed.

No one said a word. I forced myself forward, each step like walking through cement. I made it to the bathroom. Gripped the sink. Stared into the mirror.

My face was flushed. Lips dry. My eyes didn't look like mine.

I whispered the questions before anyone else could ask them.

Why didn't you ask the others to move?
Why didn't you say something?
Why didn't you protect yourself?

And then came the shame. Not just for what happened, but for what I felt.

I blamed myself. Just like every woman I'd ever interviewed out at a call who whispered, "I shouldn't have worn that," or "I should've just left."

In an instant, I was her, the younger me who froze and stayed quiet with a stranger's hand up her skirt and his friends laughing along. I was twenty-three years older and in different clothes, in a different pub, but the message was the same: You brought this on yourself.

I couldn't tell my husband David, an officer as well. He would've demanded names. Demanded consequences. And maybe, somewhere deep down, I wanted that kind of protection. But I was also terrified of what it might create. The confrontation. The drama. The fallout. I didn't want to be a problem. I didn't want to be that girl, the one who made things uncomfortable. I was finally one of them. I didn't want to disrupt that. I couldn't do anything to damage my hard-faught position.

So I said nothing.
Again.

I also knew what others might ask me..

Why didn't you stay away from him?
Why didn't you ask someone else to move?
Why didn't you say something in the moment?

I was afraid of those questions, not because I didn't know the answers, but because deep down I believed the same things. I thought it was my fault. What I couldn't face then was that the fear of those questions was really the fear of confronting my own shame.

That was the part I avoided most, not the questions themselves, but what they would force me to see about myself, that I had been carrying shame that was never really mine to hold.

I felt the embarrassment of that slap lodge in my body like a stone I couldn't swallow.

I carried that feeling all the way to the mirror.
To my home.
To my pillow.

And then I buried it, just like I had done before.

The truth is, at twenty-three and at forty-three, my body spoke

before my voice ever could.
I froze.
I stayed quiet.
I turned the blame inward.

The skirt at the pub.
The jeans at the bar.
Two decades apart.
Two different versions of me.

But the same message quietly etched itself into my bones.
This was your fault.

That's what shame does. It doesn't shout. It whispers. It twists what happened into what you somehow deserved.

And because it happened over and over, I began to believe the constant through all of it was me, that I was the problem. And when I didn't scream or fight or report it, I told myself it wasn't that bad.

But the truth is, the moment I silenced myself, it was already too much. That shame settled deep, sometimes hidden, sometimes close enough to touch.

I used to think getting older would make me stronger. And maybe it has. But strength doesn't erase the marks these moments leave behind. It just means I can finally speak what I used to swallow.

The moment you realize you aren't safe in the world, something breaks. You don't move the same after that. You don't walk out the door with the same ease or the same trust. A part of you gets left behind, the part that believed you were untouchable, the part that felt free. What's left is different. Quieter. Always just a little more on guard.

SCARED LITTLE GIRL

My son Owen called me while I was driving home from the studio. His voice carried that edge I know too well—frustration, heaviness, something restless embedded into every word. And beneath it all I could hear what he couldn't yet name: Fear.

Not panic, not terror, but the quieter, pervasive kind, the kind of fear that slowly seeps into your bones and makes you second-guess yourself. The kind I lived in for decades without ever realizing it had a name.

I gripped the steering wheel, listening as he explained the pressures at work, how he felt like he was always bracing for something to go wrong. Every clipped sentence, every rushed explanation, sounded like an echo of my own younger voice.

I wanted to tell him everything. That he was strong. That he belonged. That fear didn't have to run his life. But the truth is, he wouldn't have understood me. I know because I wouldn't have understood it either. Not back when I needed to hear it most.

Owen's voice stayed with me long after I hung up. The response on my body stayed with me too. Hearing him experience the very fears I experienced for so many years was difficult. It was hard to hear that my son was living with this and it was humbling to know that the remnants of my own fear still lingered somewhere within me.

I remember the first time someone told me I was living in fear. It wasn't a therapist. Nor a colleague. Not even my family. It was a shaman in the middle of the Brazilian jungle, who looked straight through me and said: You are just a scared little girl.

No one had ever said that to me before. And yet the second she spoke the words, I knew she was right. She saw me well before I saw myself.

Owen's words tangled with hers, years apart, worlds apart even, but carrying the same truth: Fear had been running the show. His life now. My life then.

It's an interesting thing, when something from the present immediately brings forward the past. Being able to see Owen's fears, knowing that I experienced them myself, brought me straight back to Brazil, to the moment I realized fear had been shaping me in ways I had never allowed myself to see.

I hadn't even heard the word *ayahuasca* until I read *Will* by Will Smith. He wrote about traveling into the Amazon, drinking this ancient brew with shamans, and seeing his life with a clarity he'd never known before.

The way he described the medicine as deepening his understanding of himself, in a way he had never known before, lit curiosity, intrigue, and maybe even desperation, within me.

By then, it had been two years since I'd gone off work. Therapy was helping, but I felt stuck, like I'd hit a ceiling I couldn't break through. The retreat I'd done with other first responders had been life-altering, like someone flipped a switch and my whole world now existed on a different plane. But now, I was just standing in the dark again, staring at the pieces of myself and my life, unsure how to put them back together.

They say ayahuasca calls you. That it finds you when you're ready. And maybe that's what was happening, because once I read about it, I couldn't stop thinking about it. The word itself, ayahuasca, followed me everywhere. I'd be folding laundry, driving, scrolling my phone, and suddenly it would rise up in me, telling me to look into it.

So I did.

I searched in the quiet, like I was doing something forbidden. I read articles, stories, warnings. Some people described profound healing. Others described terror. Many described both. And scattered in between were stories that scared me, women left vulnerable in unsafe ceremonies, shamans who abused their power. If I was going to do this, it couldn't be reckless.

That's when I found it, a retreat in Brazil, led by a woman who was both a shaman and a licensed psychotherapist. She spoke about integrity, safety, and integration. Not just ceremony, but what came after. She ran workshops on inner child work, the very thing I'd been struggling with in therapy. Everything about her words felt steady, safe. My heart whispered, *this is the way in.*

So I booked it.

The preparation was strict. Six weeks of cleansing the body so the medicine could work safely and deeply. No alcohol. No caffeine. No sugar. No meat. No dairy. No processed food. No medications.

On paper, it looked like deprivation. But deprivation wasn't new to me.

I used to starve myself in my modeling days, I thought the only thing that mattered was being thin. I didn't know a thing about health, about nutrition. Hunger was the goal. That gnawing emptiness in my stomach meant I was winning. Food had never been a friend. It was the thing I feared, measured, and controlled.

This time, it was different.

The rules were strict, but they weren't about punishment. They were about care. Nourishment. Every time I let go of something, it wasn't deprivation, it was intention. Eating clean and eating simply, felt less like restriction and more like preparation. Like I was making space inside myself for whatever was coming.

And for the first time in my life, food was medicine.

I didn't tell many people I was going. Not even most of my friends. It wasn't a secret. It was protection.

I knew how fast the opinions would come, "It's too dangerous." "You're going alone?" "What if something happens?" Their voices would have been full of care, but also of fear. And I didn't trust myself enough not to be swayed.

Therapy had been showing me how deep my people-pleasing ran. How quickly I let other people's voices drown out my own. How I could sit in a room with ten opinions and walk out convinced that every single one of them was right. That I was wrong.

So I held this one close.

My husband wasn't coming. My kids weren't coming. This was mine. I was choosing something just for me.

The retreat was hidden deep in the jungle. Cabins scattered among the trees. Hammocks swaying lazily on wooden decks. The air alive with birds and insects, the sounds both wild and strangely soothing.

The ceremony room was round, a simple circle with a high thatched roof and screens wrapping around the walls to keep the jungle just at the edges. It felt both open and protected, like we were inside and outside at the same time. The air moved easily through the screens, carrying the calls of insects, birds, and the layered chorus of jungle life. Inside, mattresses were laid out like petals of a flower, each with a pillow and a bucket waiting at the edge. That bucket alone made my stomach tighten, a silent reminder of what was coming.

That first night, we gathered in the circle, the air already heavy with anticipation. Outside, rain had begun to fall, soft at first, just enough that we arrived with umbrellas in hand. But even that light rain worked on my nerves, the way it tapped against the thatched roof, steady, insistent, like the sky itself was warning us something was coming.

Then she entered—the shaman. Her presence alone seemed to still the air around us. Not commanding the way I was used to in policing, not the kind of authority that demanded obedience, but something steadier. Grounded. Rooted. She carried herself like an anchor, and the moment she began to speak, I felt the edges of my nerves soften. Hers wasn't power that pressed down on you. Hers was the kind of presence that made you feel safe enough to finally let go.

She told us ayahuasca was not something to fight. That fear, if it came, could be eased by simply opening our eyes. That we were safe.

Safe. Something I hadn't felt in a long time

Before the cups of ayahuasca were passed out, the shaman asked us to speak our intentions. She told us the medicine would meet us where we were, but we had to open the door first. One by one, we each spoke our intentions aloud, some voices steady, others breaking.

And when it was my turn, my voice shook. But I said the truth: I wanted to know my purpose.
I wanted to stop people-pleasing. I wanted to release my grief for my mom and my sister.
And I wanted to let go of the shame my seventeen year old self had carried all these years.

And beneath it all, there was a question I couldn't bring myself to say out loud and was afraid to have answered, but it sat with me, pressing against me: What if the life I'm living isn't the life I'm meant to be living?

We each drank from a small cup. The brew was thick, earthy, bitter. I swallowed quickly, pressed a ginger slice to my tongue, and waited.

It wasn't long after that the rain turned harder, the steady patter swelling into something wilder. Thunder cracked like a whip. Rain pounded the roof. The jungle shrieked alive with frogs and insects, shadows shifting just beyond the light.

And then the medicine hit.

It started in my toes, a warm electric tingle that climbed my legs and wrapped itself around my chest until my whole body vibrated. My breath caught. My hands gripped the blanket. Around me, voices broke into sobs, buckets filled, the sound of retching echoing. And still I told myself: Not me, not here, not now.

But ayahuasca doesn't care about pride.

The purge came, not through my mouth, but through my body, through every cell, every bone. I dissolved into the floor, into the earth.

And suddenly I wasn't Erin anymore.

I was a rock. Heavy. Cold. Forgotten. Buried in the soil. Rain falling on me. Centuries passing over me. The terror of being stuck forever. Immobile. Not existing.

I wanted it to stop. I wanted to claw my way back. But I couldn't move. Couldn't speak.

The shaman's words found me in the dark, don't fight it. Be curious. You are safe.

I clung to that last word as if it were the only solid thing left in the room. Safe. I repeated it over and over, even as my body trembled. Slowly, almost without realizing, the weight began to lift.

By the time the storm outside eased, something inside me had eased too. I wasn't sure how long I'd been lying there, only that when I opened my eyes, the sky beyond the screens was beginning to pale. Birds were singing, steady and bright, like they hadn't just witnessed me unravel.

I walked back to my cabin slowly, every step unsteady, like I was still carrying the weight of the night. Nothing around me looked different, but I did. My body felt hollowed out, my skin too thin, my chest still echoing with fear.

I crawled beneath the mosquito netting, pulled out my journal, and forced my hand to move before the memories slipped away, the rock, the storm, the rain that wasn't rain. Writing was the only way I knew to tether myself to what had happened, proof that it was real.

I didn't feel healed. I didn't feel whole. I felt stripped. Raw. Like layers I'd worn my whole life had been ripped away and now there was nothing left to hide behind. Maybe that was the point.

And I was just beginning.

Days blurred into a rhythm, ceremony, rest, ceremony again. Some nights were gentler. Others hollowed me out. In between, I floated in the pond, scribbled words into my journal, or sat with the group as we quietly unraveled together. People cried openly, their bodies shaking with release, and no one rushed to stop it. No one said, "Don't cry." Tears were allowed. Grief was allowed. I started to wonder what it would feel like to stop protecting people from mine.

One evening at dinner, I tried to explain myself to the retreat's shaman. I spilled everything, the resentment I carried toward policing, the anger lodged in my bones, the way I didn't know who I was without the badge. I circled the same questions over and over. Who am I? What do I do with my life?

She listened, silent. Then she tilted her head, her Argentinian accent wrapping around a sentence that made everything I thought I knew about myself collapse.

"You are just a scared little girl."

The words plummeted like the ground giving way beneath me. Everything in me went quiet, waiting for her to soften them, explain them. She didn't. She just let them hang there, sharp and alive, while my mind rebelled and my chest burned with recognition.

I wanted to deny it. Argue. But I couldn't. Because the truth is, she was right. For decades, I thought shame was the thing that shaped me. That moment at seventeen with my dad. The secret I carried. The identity I built around hiding it. I thought shame was the driver.

But fear had been right there all along. Fear had been the current underneath everything. Fear of not being enough. Fear of being left. Fear of life collapsing if I let go. Fear was shame's companion.

And in that circle of strangers, in the middle of the jungle, a woman had named it before I could.

"You are just a scared little girl."

She didn't just see me, she exposed me.

That night, lying under the mosquito net with the jungle alive around me, I finally let the words settle. I wasn't just ashamed. I wasn't just grieving. I wasn't just uncertain. I was scared. And maybe I always had been.

But now, I could see it. I could name it. And naming it was the beginning of finally letting it go.

SOMETHING
TO
BE
PROUD
OF

There was something about the uniform that made me feel different. Like slipping into it transformed me into someone who belonged. Someone who had earned the right to take up space in places most people were just passing through.

When I became a flight attendant, I thought I'd finally landed something respectable. This was a job people admired. One that made strangers light up when they asked what I did for work. "Oh wow, you must love it!" they'd say, eyes wide with curiosity, imagining glamour, freedom, and endless travel.

And I'd smile, because they were right, I did love it. It was every bit as exciting and fulfilling as they imagined, and I felt lucky to be living it.

It was the first job I'd had where I didn't feel the need to justify it. Where I didn't brace for judgment. Where people looked at me like I had my life together.

And for a while, I believed it.

This was my first legit job. Not a job I was hiding. Not a role I was ashamed of. Not something temporary while I figured out what I really wanted to do. This felt like something to be proud of. Something that counted. It felt like progress. Like proof that I was doing something right. Like I was becoming someone.

But it was still a performance. The compliments were classier. The setting was elevated. But the script was the same.

Be charming.
Be composed.
Be beautiful.
Be small.

And maybe, if I could do all that perfectly, I'd be seen as good enough.

Training was intense, weeks of emergency drills, tests, evacuation slides, and memorizing safety procedures. I hadn't studied for anything since high school. I was terrified I wouldn't pass. I stayed up late each night reviewing every manual, afraid I'd miss something important. Afraid I wouldn't belong.

I'll never forget my first day in uniform. The fabric was stiff, the heels pinched, and yet I held myself taller than I felt inside. Each button I fastened was less about confidence and more about survival — as though if I looked the part long enough, maybe I'd finally believe I belonged.

The terminal buzzed with that familiar pre-flight buzz, rolling suitcases clicking over tile, announcements crackling overhead. But when we stepped out in formation, heads turned. Conversations paused. Passengers' eyes followed us, curiosity mingled with admiration, like we were part of a world they couldn't quite touch.

Underneath the uniform something unexpected was happening. I felt professional. Important. Needed. I was relied on for safety, for structure, for the reassurance that everything would be okay. And no other job had ever given me that kind of responsibility. For the first time, I wasn't invisible. I was part of something, and I mattered.

"Welcome, I hope you enjoy your flight," I said, smiling broadly as though I was welcoming a friend to my home. It felt like slipping into a role the world had written for me, polished, composed, untouchable. And I leaned into it. Because behind the mystique, I still felt like a girl terrified of failing, afraid I didn't belong. The uniform masked all of that. To them, I wasn't Erin fumbling through fear. I was a confident and capable flight attendant, steady and serene, a piece of the sky.

For those first few years, I wore the uniform not just as clothing, but as a promise to myself, that I was enough, that I mattered, that I could perform the role of being seen.

Not every part of the flight was a performance, but even behind the scenes I was playing a role. Once in the air, we changed into "galley shoes", flats we wore behind the curtain, where the real work began. And here I would become efficient Erin, productive Erin, adaptable Erin. There was always a deeper need to not just be good at my job but to prove my worthiness. Then we'd prepare for landing, stepping back into the performance and our heels. Lipstick reapplied. A ritual we all knew by heart.

"Lips for landing," we'd say, laughing quietly in the galley. And we'd do it. Because that's what was expected. That was the performance. There were moments of joy, layovers in new cities, crew pub nights, spontaneous laughter that made the long hours and constant travel feel lighter.

There was a night in Dublin when we told a table of men we were Canada's national beach volleyball team. None of us were tall enough, tan enough, or athletic enough for the lie, but that was half the fun. We could be anyone, weave any tale. We laughed so hard our cheeks hurt. It was ridiculous. And it was exactly what we needed to make the job feel a little less heavy.

Because not every moment was lipstick, heels, and banter between peers and passengers. I learned quickly that turbulence wasn't just in the sky—it found its way into us, too. It lived in our bodies, in the ache of muscles that never fully rested, in the fog of too many time zones, in the quiet fears we packed alongside our uniforms. We carried them home after each trip, even when no one else could see them.

Sometimes it was a missed approach, the sudden lurch of the plane as we climbed again, passengers gripping their armrests. Sometimes it was a hard landing that rattled the cabin and left our hearts pounding long after the seatbelt sign turned off. And sometimes it was worse— like an emergency slide deploying without warning, the deafening crack of the door giving way, the kind of moment that made you realize how quickly things could spiral.

We were trained for these scenarios, drilled until the motions became muscle memory. But training doesn't prepare you for the way fear moves through your body when it's real—when the weight of hundreds of lives feels like it's balanced in your hands.

I'll never forget Cuba. Our purser had gone to open the door after taxiing to the gate—having the briefest of moments when she was working on auto-pilot and not fully aware of the timing—but the door was still armed, not cleared to be opened yet. In an instant, her body stiffened, pressing all her weight against it, panic written across her face. Her knuckles were white against the handle, arms trembling, and I could feel my own pulse in my throat as I stepped toward her.

"You have to get her off that door," the captain urgently and forcefully told me. "It has power assist. It's going to drag her out."

And I did. I wrapped my arms around her and pulled her back just before the slide exploded, slamming into the stairs truck with a deafening boom.

She kept whispering, "I'm fired. I can always go back to bartending. I'm fired."

I knew that panic. That fear of being found out. Of being unworthy. Replaceable.

We were trained for emergencies, but nothing trains you for what it feels like to be responsible for so many lives, and to know that one mistake, one moment of acting on auto-pilot, could change everything, for all of them.

Sometimes the scariest moments weren't even in the air.

After one long-haul flight, a single male passenger had struck up conversation with me mid-flight—passengers were often friendly, and chatting was part of the job. At one point, while I was restocking the lavatory, I noticed him sitting right outside the door, watching me. His eyes lingered a little too long, but I was used to that. Men stared. It wasn't unusual. I brushed it off.

As we landed and passengers began to deplane, I saw that he was still in his seat, waiting. It wasn't unheard of, there was always someone who preferred to be last. I didn't think much about it until I grabbed my bag and realized he was watching me closely.

The rest of the crew had gone ahead, and I was a few steps behind when I heard footsteps fall in sync with mine. Too close. Too deliberate. The sound of my heels against the tile suddenly felt sharp, each step echoing in the empty jet bridge. My stomach tightened.

I headed toward the elevator, but at the last second, I changed to go up the escalator instead. If I stepped inside, he'd follow, and we'd be trapped together in a small metal box. The thought made my skin prickle. I quickened my pace to catch up to the pilot and purser, leaning in to whisper what was happening.

Without hesitation, the pilot turned and approached him, calm but firm. The man froze, looking stunned, as if he genuinely believed I had invited this attention, that following me was welcome.

He left. But the feeling didn't.

Later, alone in my hotel room, I double-locked the door, left the bathroom light on, and wedged my suitcase against the frame like a barricade. I lay there, listening to footsteps in the hallway, the low wheeze of the air conditioner, every creak and shift of the building, doors slamming down the hall.

This was the part no one saw. The side of travel that never made it into the glossy photos or romantic daydreams. The danger that lurked, disguised as ordinary moments.

People saw the heels, the glamour, the travel, and I loved those parts, I truly did. But I was beginning to understand it wasn't only that.

Behind the polished smiles and perfect lipstick, there was a shadow side. Nights when adrenaline still coursed through you long after the flight was over. Moments when safety felt fragile, even on solid ground. A loneliness that crept in quietly, no matter how full the cabin had been hours before.

And soon, all of it would be eclipsed by a moment that would change the course of my life.

September 11, 2001. I wasn't flying that day. But the phone rang early that morning. It was my mother-in-law. "Are you okay?" she asked. I didn't understand, until I turned on the TV and watched, in real time, as the second plane hit.

And the world stilled and shifted.

Flights were grounded.
Borders closed.
Fear flooded every gate, every airport, every cockpit.
Security changed.

The fun parts of the job—visiting the flight deck, chatting happily with the crew—they vanished overnight. Doors locked, not just figuratively, but literally. Before, we used to slip into the cockpit mid-flight, sink into the jump seat for a few minutes, chat with the pilots, stretch our legs, and catch our breath. It was a small escape from the constant sounds of service. But now, the flight deck door stayed shut from takeoff to landing, sealed tight. Only the captain and first officer were allowed inside. That easy camaraderie was gone.

Passengers seemed different too. More on edge. Nervous in a way they hadn't been before and who could blame them? Every glance felt heavier, every request tinged with a kind of unspoken fear. The cabin felt more serious, more guarded. Smiles hesitant and strained. The air itself more pressurized. Even the sound of the engines sounded different, lower somehow, like the whole world had shifted frequency.

The magic drained away, quietly and completely.

The airline tried to hold on, but what was happening behind the scenes was kept from us, so we didn't see it coming. It was a slow unraveling. Loads were down, and the company was bleeding money.

Bills weren't being paid, including the airport landing fees that kept us in the air. None of us knew just how bad it was until one day, the consequences arrived without warning.

Planes started being seized on the tarmac. Crews, mid-trip, were suddenly stranded in cities with no flights home. The stories trickled through in disbelief, whispered between shifts, until the truth became impossible to ignore. The doors were closing. We were bankrupt.

By the time I could reapply somewhere else, I was pregnant with Owen. I didn't have enough hours for maternity leave, so I stayed home.

The wings that once made me feel like I could soar, were gone. No goodbye. No closure. Just… gone.

And with them went the woman I thought I was—the one in lipstick and heels, walking the aisle like she owned it. But that wasn't freedom, not really. It was me performing. Smiling when I was supposed to. Saying the right lines. Pretending I wasn't terrified someone would notice I didn't actually belong there. The uniform made me look steady, but inside I was still bracing.

When the airline shut down and I found out I was pregnant, everything went quiet. No more safety demos to half-listening passengers. No more lipstick touch-ups in the crew room. Just me. And the tiny heartbeat inside me reminding me that something new was beginning.

Not glamorous. Not admired. Not applauded.

But finally, real.

BREAKING POINT

I used to drive to the police station every day with my shoulders curled around my ears. Not because of traffic or what was happening on the road itself. It was me, my body locked into vigilance, stiff as though expecting the world might collapse any second. Coffee in the cupholder, radio low, stomach unsettled. I was always bracing for something but I never knew what.

Today, I'm driving the same highway. Same turns, same exits. But this time, I'm headed toward my studio, and bulldog puppies are waiting for me. I've got my yoga mat in the trunk. My shoulders are where they're meant to be. My nervous system isn't on high alert. My muscles aren't bracing for what comes next. I'm actually looking forward to it. Music is loud and vibrant. The wind tangles my hair through the open window.

And the contrast… is beautiful.

Because back then, I loved my job. At least, I thought I did. I was proud of it. I was good at it. It made me feel like I mattered. But somewhere in all that pride, somewhere between the reports and the uniforms and the late-night shifts, I lost myself.

Policing wasn't just a career. It was my attempt at stability. At proving I could do hard things. At being the one who kept everything afloat when my marriage was crumbling and my kids needed security. My ex wouldn't change careers or step up financially, so I had to. And policing seemed like the answer.

In many ways, it was.

It gave me benefits, a steady paycheck, and structure. But more than that, it gave me recognition. And recognition felt like oxygen to someone who'd spent a lifetime trying to earn her place in the world.

I approached the job the same way I approached everything else in my life, head down, do more, be the best. Don't say no. Learn fast. Don't complain. Make sure everyone notices how hard you're working, even if it's killing you.

I wasn't aware I was doing this. I just knew I wanted to be seen. To be respected. To be appreciated. Isn't that what everyone wants?

Looking back now, I can see what I was really doing: trying to outrun my self-doubt. Trying to earn love through performance. Trying to prove something.

When I first joined the traffic unit on a temporary assignment, I started on the enforcement side — and I loved it. Stopping cars, pulling over impaired drivers, being out on the road. That kind of police work lit me up.

But management had other plans. With retirements looming, they needed more reconstructionists — the specialists who took the lead on fatal collisions. And because my temporary assignment came up for renewal every three months, I knew I couldn't really say no when they began steering me in that direction.

Reconstructionists carried prestige. They were the ones who could take shattered glass, skid marks, and twisted steel and piece together the story of what happened. Their work carried weight in courtrooms. They were seen as the smart ones, the experts. And part of me wanted that. I wanted to be seen as capable of the kind of work that set you apart.

But deep down, I was terrified. Math and physics had always been my worst subjects. Numbers blurred, formulas slipped through my fingers. Enforcement felt natural. Collision work felt like a spotlight on everything I didn't know. Outwardly, I leaned in. Inwardly, I braced for the day they'd realize what I already feared: that I wasn't smart enough to belong there.

Still, I did what they asked. They put me through the in-house recon-struction course, and somehow, I passed. On paper, I looked capable. Inside, it felt like a narrow escape. But that wasn't the end. To actually secure a permanent spot as a reconstructionist in the traffic unit, I had to pass an outside accreditation exam — a full day of high-stakes testing in physics and math. It was notorious for failure. And the thought of it made me sick.

I studied relentlessly — binders stacked on the kitchen table, notes taped to the walls, coffee going cold beside me. My kids would walk past pages of equations that meant nothing to them but carried all my hopes. The day of the exam felt like going into battle. Twelve hours under fluorescent lights, formulas swimming until they blurred. I walked out convinced I had failed. And I had.

The failure gutted me. But I told myself I'd try again. So I doubled down, grinding harder, determined to prove I could do it.

Just as I was regaining momentum with my studying, management told me to stop. For the first time in five years, positions had come up in the traffic unit for enforcement officers. These weren't automatic positions—they were filled through an application and competition process, open to any officer in the service. Management framed it as the easier path, more straightforward than the accreditation exam.

So I set the binders aside and focused on preparing my application, believing this was finally my chance at permanence.

Then, without warning, the positions were canceled. No explanation. Just gone. One of the managers pulled me aside and quietly broke the news. "Go back to studying for your accreditation", they said, like it was no big deal.

So I picked the binders back up, even though my confidence was already shaken. I told myself this was my only way forward.

But just as I rescheduled my rewrite, the enforcement positions came back again. Management urged me to pivot once more—cancel the exam, forget the studying, focus on applying for the traffic enforcement positions again. "This is your way in," they said.

And then, just before I could send in my application, an email landed in my inbox. The traffic positions were canceled again. No warning. No conversation. Just a subject line that flattened months of work.

That was the moment something in me broke. I wasn't a person to them, I was a pawn—moved around depending on what the unit needed that week. Each shift in direction sent me spiraling, and the message became clearer every time: my future wasn't mine to decide.

The push and pull shredded me. Study. Stop. Resume. Application. Cancel. Study. Over and over again. It was like trying to build a foundation on shifting ground. And in that chaos, I started to lose trust. In them. In myself. In the whole system.

I did my best to refocus. I rescheduled the accreditation exam and forced myself back into the binders. The rewrite was brutal, twelve straight hours of math equations and technical scenarios that felt designed to expose every weakness. By the time I walked out, I was hollow.

But the exam didn't end when I left the room. My mind replayed it on a loop, racing through what I should have written, what piece of evidence I might have missed, what formula I should have chosen. Nights blurred into half-sleep, my body exhausted but my brain stuck in overdrive. Rest felt impossible. Relaxation unreachable. I was haunted by the fear that I'd failed again.

Weeks later, my sergeant asked to meet. We pulled up window-to-window, and the heaviness in her face hit me before the words did. A rush of heat spread through my chest before I even knew what she was going to say.

Her eyes were kind, but uneasy. She was carrying something she didn't want to hand over. I felt it in my body before I heard it, a sharp constriction in my chest, hollowness spreading in my stomach, breath turning shallow.

"They're not renewing your temporary assignment next month," she said.

The words landed with more force than any failed exam or canceled posting, because this wasn't just about a job. It was about two years of pushing past exhaustion, of studying when my body begged for rest, of missing dinners and moments at home. It was about proving I belonged, stitching my identity to the work. And now, with one line, it all came undone.

I don't remember the drive home.

What I do remember is walking through my front door and collapsing on the floor, the sobs ripping out of me, louder and more primal than anything I'd ever heard from my own body. My knees hit the tile, my hands pressed against the cold floor, and I howled. Years of swallowed pain poured out all at once.

It terrified me.

That moment felt like failure. Like I had lost everything I'd been working for. But now I know it was the beginning of freedom.

Because my sergeant, bless her, had seen it all along. The tears, the exhaustion, the heaviness that clung to me every day. She tried to reach me, but I was deaf to it then. Her voice couldn't compete with the one in my head that said, keep going. And in the end, she was the one left to deliver the news, carrying what the decision-makers were too afraid to say themselves.

I had built my entire identity on the belief that if I worked hard enough, performed well enough, said yes enough, I would finally be whole. And for a while, it worked. I got praised. Promoted. I was "the one they called." The one who never said no.

But deep down, I was starving—for recognition, for belonging, for love I didn't know how to give myself.

I wasn't sleeping. My hair was falling out. My chest ached. My legs felt like lead. And I kept brushing it off, telling myself I was just tired, just stressed, just in a rough patch. But I wasn't. I was sick from the inside out.

And policing only fueled it. It rewarded my over-functioning, my self-abandonment, my willingness to bleed for belonging.

The saddest part? I did it to myself.

Whether they meant to or not, they fed the wound in me that kept asking: Am I good enough yet?

I didn't know the answer to that myself so I kept sacrificing.

Until my body answered for me.

Crashing to the floor that day wasn't the end. It was the doorway. The only thing that could strip me of the illusion that performance was love, that sacrifice was worth, that saying yes would ever save me.

I believe policing was placed in my path not to fulfill me, but to break me open. To strip away everything I thought would keep me safe until I had no choice but to see the truth.

That I didn't need recognition to matter. I didn't need perfection to belong. I didn't need the uniform to prove my worth.

And now, years later, as I calmly drive the same highway toward a yoga studio filled with puppies and laughter, with the music loud and windows down, I realize, it wasn't the end of my career. It was the beginning of my freedom.

NOTHING, AND EVERYTHING, TO DO WITH ME

A re you Erin?"

The simple question sliced through the quiet of that morning.

I was sitting in my car in David's driveway, waiting for him so we could leave on a road trip. The engine idled beneath me, the radio playing quietly in the background. From inside the car I could hear the clink of his keys as he locked his front door.

We had been together for three years at this point and I still got butterflies whenever we planned time away, just the two of us. The thought of long stretches of highway, music playing, nowhere to be but together, it still thrilled me. We still had that magic between us.

I noticed a car approaching. It slowed as it drew closer, then stopped beside me. A woman rolled her window down and leaned out.

"Are you Erin?" she asked.

"Yes," I said, polite but already bracing. Her tone and demeanor filled me with tension. Something was wrong.

"I've been dating David for the last two years. I thought you should know."

The air around me vanished. My fingers went cold on the steering wheel. My stomach dropped out of me. David was walking toward us now, close enough to hear every word. His jaw was tight, but his voice was flat, "Are you happy now?" he said to her.

She drove away.

Nausea rose so fast it stole my breath. My heart pounded so loudly it drowned out the world. My mind scrambled for explanations, for math that would make it make sense. Two years. We'd been together for three.

And yet, under the shock, there was relief. The unease I'd been living with finally had a name. All the little things I couldn't quite explain, the way his phone was always on silent, always close to him, never left out of reach. Even at home, it stayed in his pocket or turned facedown nearby. The excuses not to visit. The distance between us I couldn't quite explain

But like for many of us, my body sensed something was going on, even if I wasn't ready to consciously face it. My stomach would twist when the phone buzzed at odd hours, my chest would tighten when he pulled away without explanation. My intuition, that small voice I'd spent years dismissing, had whispered all along that something wasn't right. But I didn't trust it. I ignored it. I convinced myself it was paranoia, or neediness, or insecurity.

Even in that moment, when everything lined up, when my gut was screaming: *See! You were right*, I still didn't fully lean into what was right in front of me. It would take me many more years and a lot of therapy before I began to trust the wisdom in my body, to understand that the signals it sent me weren't weakness or oversensitivity—they were truth.

But truth doesn't make the pain easier. My body went into overdrive, heart hammering, hands trembling, my skin buzzing like I'd been plugged into a socket. My nervous system didn't know if it should fight, flee, or collapse.

I looked at him and the only words that came out were, "Let's go."

It sounds impossible, I know. My entire world had just been turned upside down in the span of a single sentence, and yet I still put the car in drive. I still left for that road trip with him. I still played the part of the girlfriend heading off on an adventure, even as my insides felt like glass.

The sound of our seatbelts clicking into place was louder than it should have been, almost jarring in the silence between us. My hands white-knuckled the steering wheel, rigid, while my mind spun with questions I struggled to form into words. I pulled out of the driveway numb, my body moving through motions that no longer made sense.

We drove. Mile after mile, I ricocheted between extremes. I cried so hard I could barely see the road. I screamed into the space between us. I laughed in that too-loud, unstable way that only comes when your body has no idea where to land. The highway stretched out in front of us like nothing had happened, but inside me, everything had.

I met David the February after my mom died. It was her birthday, and I couldn't bear the thought of being alone, so I went to visit my dad. His wife, also an officer, set me up with a ride-along.

David wasn't even the officer I was supposed to go with, but plans changed, and he ended up taking me out. I remember sliding into the passenger seat of the cruiser, the smell of summer air still clinging to me, the static of the radio filling the silence between us. He had an ease about him, confident, quick to smile and for a few hours, I didn't feel like the grieving daughter or the single mom barely keeping it together. I just felt… seen.

We drove for hours through quiet streets, talking about everything, our kids, our families, our lives. It flowed so easily. By the time the shift ended, he had my email, and before long the messages started.

He was ending a marriage, preparing to transfer twenty-two hours north to a small town he'd never even seen, ironically, near the same town where I had grown up. It should have been the end before it started. But we both wanted to believe it could work. Somehow, we decided it would.

In the beginning, there was nothing to make me doubt him. He was attentive, steady, and proved himself worthy of trust. That's the man he truly is at his core. It wasn't until he moved north, living alone for the first time in his life, that the edges began to frey. Something about that distance, that isolation and leaving his children, began to change things.

From the beginning, distance was part of our story.

We learned more about each other through late-night phone calls, weekend visits, and short trips whenever we could manage them. When the boys were with their dad, I'd fly north. Sometimes I'd drive hours on my own just to squeeze in a few days together.

There was joy in the adventure of it, road trips, new places, laughter filling the quiet between long stretches of highway. But there was unease, too. Subtle things I couldn't quite put my finger on. His tone sometimes shifted when I would question something, little things my gut noticed, even when I reasoned with myself to ignore them.

And I did what I had always done, I bent myself to fit. At the time, I didn't recognize it for what it was. I told myself I was just being flexible, supportive, the kind of partner who could roll with anything. But looking back, I see how I was contorting myself into a mold of the woman I thought he wanted. Fun but easygoing. Strong but not demanding. Loyal but never too much. Fear was driving me. Fear of losing him. Fear of being alone. And maybe, somewhere deep in my body, I already sensed that something wasn't right. Subconsciously, I think I believed that if I could be everything—perfect, desirable, effortless, then he wouldn't need or want anyone else.

I was hired onto the same police service he worked for. The boys and I moved to a town two and a half hours closer, believing that closing the distance between us might fix what felt broken. But it didn't. If anything, the gap inside me only grew wider.

He made excuses not to come to my house on his days off. I was always the one driving, the one chasing. My heart ached with the distance, even when the geography was smaller. One weekend, after I'd moved closer, I stayed at David's place while my boys were visiting their dad. It was one of the first nights I had slept there. We had just climbed into bed and turned off the light. The house was quiet—the kind of rural silence that usually feels safe. And then, all of a sudden…

BANG. BANG. BANG.

The pounding rattled the back door so hard it felt like the hinges might snap. My body went rigid. My heart hammered in my ears. We froze in the dark, pressed together, listening.

"What is that?" I whispered, my voice barely audible.

"I don't know," David said, his tone clipped, eyes straining toward the sound.

Then silence.

And then it started again, louder. Against the window this time. BANG. BANG. BANG. Like someone was circling the house.

"I don't like this," I said, clutching the blanket tighter.

"Me neither," he muttered, reaching for his phone. "I'm calling the detachment."

David called it in, and soon an officer drove out to the property. He went outside to meet them, the two of them searching the yard while I stayed inside, too terrified to move, every nerve in my body lit up.

The next morning, I met a childhood friend for breakfast. My voice was still shaky as I described the pounding at the door, the banging on the windows, the way my body refused to relax even after the officer left. He listened quietly, then leaned forward.

"Erin… do you think it could've been another woman?" I blinked at him, confused. "No… I thought maybe it was someone angry at David from work. He arrests people all day. It could've been anyone."

He shook his head slowly. "I don't think so. If it was random, they wouldn't pound like that. Not at the door, then the windows, circling the house like they knew you were inside."

I wanted to argue. I wanted him to be wrong. But he kept going, gently, firmly. "Your car was in the driveway. Whoever it was knew you were there. Erin… it makes a lot of sense that it was someone else. Someone who didn't want to find you in his house."

The words didn't just land, they lodged. My stomach turned to stone. I couldn't un-hear them. And, again, my body knew, before my mind was willing to accept it. Part of me knew he was right.

Because the truth is, I didn't have proof then. All I had was a gut feeling. And while today I know my gut is always right, back then it was something I didn't understand. My body would whisper, my stomach would twist, my chest would tighten, but my mind would dismiss it all. The two were so detached from one another that I couldn't recognize intuition for what it was. I only knew discomfort, unease, and the ache of something I couldn't name.

And the alternative felt unbearable. The idea of being in my isolated town with two young boys, navigating a brand-new career in policing on my own, without him—even from a distance, was too much to bear. I couldn't face the silence of those nights. I couldn't face the thought of holding everything together completely alone.

But on that road trip, I demanded answers, my voice sharp and frantic in the car.

When we reached our destination, I grabbed a bottle of Jägermeister and poured shot after shot, each one punctuated with the same refrain: How could I have been so stupid? Of course he cheated. How could I not have seen it? Until finally, I passed out.

The next morning, and every morning after, I wanted to bring it up again. I wanted him to tell me more, to give me a reason, to make it make sense. But he never did. All he ever said was I don't know. At the time, I thought he was being evasive, protecting me from the truth I feared most, that I wasn't enough. That if I had been prettier, funnier, better, he wouldn't have strayed.

But every time I asked, his patience thinned. His voice sharpened.

Eventually, anger replaced answers. And so I learned the cost of asking was higher than the cost of silence. He taught me that talking about it was more painful than swallowing it. So I stopped asking. I bottled it up. I learned to carry the questions alone.

After years of long-distance, we finally put in for transfers at the same time, each of us uncertain but willing to see what might happen. As fate would have it, we landed at neighboring detachments, which meant, for the first time, we could build a home together. We bought a house, moved in, and for a while I believed proximity would fix what distance had frayed.

But the opposite happened. Living together stripped away the buffer of distance, and suddenly the cracks were everywhere. I struggled to get past the betrayal, the lies, the gnawing suspicion that never really left me. My body still flinched with old memories. And David struggled too, caught in his own endless loop, reliving what he had done, drowning in shame and guilt he couldn't outrun.

We did this dance of me twisting myself into impossible shapes, desperate to prove I was "enough"; him withdrawing, defensive, his silence heavy with things he didn't fully understand himself. We cycled between closeness and collapse. Nights that felt tender, hopeful. Mornings when I'd wake to the pit in my stomach again. Every time I thought we were steady, the ground shifted.

I kept asking myself the same punishing questions: What's wrong with me? Why wasn't I enough? How could I make him choose me, fully? I thought if I was fun enough, forgiving enough, loving enough, maybe he would stay. Maybe he would stop. But the more I contorted myself, the further I seemed to slip away from myself.

Eventually, I realized the only way forward was therapy. At first, David resisted, he didn't want to go there, didn't want to face the parts of himself he'd worked so hard to avoid. But when he realized I wasn't bluffing, that without it, our relationship would not survive, he began to show up. Hesitant at first. Then more fully.

It was messy. Ugly, at times—many times. I had to face the ways I'd abandoned myself in order to hold the relationship together. He had to face how his choices weren't just betrayals of me, but betrayals of himself.

In therapy years later, a counselor asked me, "Erin, what if his betrayal wasn't about you at all?"
I froze. For years I had made myself sick trying to answer what I lacked. But with that question I saw the truth: It had never been about me.

He wasn't searching outside of us because I wasn't enough. He was searching because he couldn't sit with himself. The silence was too much. The TV wasn't loud enough. The alcohol wasn't strong enough. He was trying to outrun the parts of himself he couldn't face.

It was messy. It was heartbreaking. It was complicated.

The man David is today is not the man I lived with through those years of betrayal and distance. The man I first met in that cruiser all those years ago—the one who was kind, attentive, open—that is him. That is his truest nature. What came in between were the years that nearly broke us both: the guilt he carried for leaving his family, the shame of his choices, and the desperate ways he tried to soothe the ache inside himself—with other women, with numbing, with chaos. And for me, those years became a different kind of prison. Years of bending. Of doubting. Of pushing down the voice in my gut that begged me to listen. Years of carrying pain that was never mine alone to hold. Of swallowing betrayals, one after another, until silence became survival. I wasn't healing. I was disappearing.

David didn't fully understand his own "why" until much later. For years, he couldn't face it. But life has a way of forcing us into the places we resist most. The same unit at work that had broken me, eventually broke him too. The overwork, the trauma, the endless stress, it all caught up. And when he finally went off work himself, when his body and mind gave out, he had no choice but to stop running.

That was the beginning of his own unwinding. The moment the noise went quiet enough for him to finally hear what he'd been avoiding could he start to see the truth. Why he lied, why he strayed, why silence was unbearable unless he filled it with chaos. His healing didn't begin with admitting what he did, it began with understanding why he did it. And this all had to come from him, come at a time when he was ready to do the work and really become honest with himself.

Therapy gave him words for the shame he once buried. Introspection taught him to face the silence he used to fill with noise. Slowly, the void no longer needed chaos. And in that reckoning, he began to heal.

And so did I.

But healing wasn't just about us as a couple. It was about each of us learning to turn inward. For so long, I thought if I just became who he wanted, he would love me. And for so long, he thought if he kept chasing approval outside of himself, he would finally feel whole. Neither of us realized that what we were searching for in each other, or in other people, was really what we had to find inside ourselves.

I had to learn to love myself. To see that the most worthy version of me isn't the one who shrinks, who bends, who performs. It's the one I am when I'm real, unfiltered, honest, whole. And he had to learn that too. That his worth wasn't in numbing the silence or filling the emptiness with distraction, but in learning to sit with himself.

We both stopped looking for others to fill the void.
And slowly, we began to fill it ourselves.

But healing changed me. It changed us. And somehow, through all of it, I learned to love him again, but differently this time. Not the man I imagined. Not the man I wished he could be. But the man he is now, one who has faced his shadows, as I've faced mine. The love I carry for him today isn't built on illusions or what-ifs. It's rooted in truth. In who we both became once we stopped running from ourselves.

That's the thing about love. Sometimes it doesn't save you from yourself. Sometimes it holds up a mirror until you can no longer look away.

I believe now that we were brought together for this reason, not just to love each other, but to heal ourselves. The pain, the betrayal, the silence, the chaos… as much as I wish it could have been easier, I don't think either of us would have been forced to face our own demons without it.

He needed to see the wreckage of his choices to finally confront the shame he carried. And I needed to sit in the raw ache of not being "enough" until I realized that I always was.

It wasn't neat. It wasn't easy. But it was necessary.

And if you're brave enough, sometimes you find your way through. Together.

STARTING PLACE

The day I left work in a fog of tears and disbelief marked the beginning of the end. Not just of my career as I knew it, but of the version of me I had barely been holding together for decades.

Now I can see that what came next was the beginning of healing, but at the time it didn't feel like that. It felt like everything stopped. Instantly. Like someone had flipped a switch. The momentum, the adrenaline, the years of pushing—it all vanished in a single moment.

And then, there was nothing. No fight left in me. No strength to pretend.

The next morning, I opened my eyes and couldn't quite name what I felt. Not sadness. Not exhaustion. Just emptiness. My thoughts were dull, moving through a fog I couldn't clear. I drifted to the couch, turned on Netflix, and let the noise blur out the world. The sun poured through the windows, steady and unbothered, but it felt far away—belonging to another world I could see but not touch.

My dogs scratched at the door, still faithful to routine, but even opening it felt like climbing a mountain. That became my rhythm: couch to bed, bed to couch. No appetite. No motivation. Just silence.

My husband David was home for a few days on his scheduled days off. Like me, he worked in the traffic unit, but his rank and gender gave him a protection I never had. A respect I couldn't access. I didn't resent him for it, but I also didn't know how to let him in.

Don't get me wrong—David was wonderful. Supportive, deeply saddened by what had happened. But he didn't know how to help me. And the truth was, I didn't know either. How could he know what I needed when I couldn't even name what was happening to me?

When he left for work, the house got heavier. I'd stand at the door after he walked out and crumble. Rage, sorrow, shame, confusion— emotions without names or direction. He'd come home and try to talk about his day, and I couldn't take it. I remember snapping once: "Stop talking about work. I can't hear it anymore." He stopped. But then so did everything else.

He went silent. And suddenly, I was convinced he was hiding something. That they were talking about me. That there was a plan, a target on my back. I spiraled into paranoia so intense it didn't matter that I knew it wasn't rational. I felt it in my bones.

Sleep became impossible. I'd crash from exhaustion and then jolt awake, heart racing, brain on fire. Crash scenes. Unfinished reports. Screeching tires. My own screaming heart. My doctor prescribed anti-anxiety meds. They dulled the edges eventually, but in those first weeks, I was volatile. Crying uncontrollably. Snapping at nothing. Unrecognizable even to myself.

Letters from work started trickling in, each one like a paper cut. Not updates, not support—just demands. Clinical forms, medical notes, proof that I was still unwell enough to be off. Piece by piece, they dismantled the identity I had sacrificed so much to build. My phone, my laptop, my equipment—all gone. And with every cardboard envelope, my body panicked before I even tore it open. I wasn't a person anymore. I was a policy. A file to be managed.

When the texts followed—"Hang in there," a monkey emoji, "let us know if we can help"—they didn't feel like kindness. They felt like surveillance. Gaslighting. Especially from someone who had already put in writing that I'd left because I "didn't get my way." Every buzz of my phone set off alarms in my body. My chest tightened, my hands shook, I couldn't breathe. I begged for it to stop. I asked for help. But the answer was always the same: policy. Protocol over pain.

And that's when I realized—I was utterly alone inside a system that claimed to care. I was unraveling, invisible, with no map forward. I needed something—someone—that wasn't checking a box or following standard operating procedures. I needed a lifeline. That's when therapy entered the picture. My way out of the fog. The first sign that maybe, I was more than paperwork and policy. Maybe I was still human, after all.

And then, finally, the appointment with the psychologist came—the lifeline I'd been waiting on for weeks. At last, I would sit across from someone who might understand, someone who could help me make sense of what I couldn't untangle on my own. That appointment would be the first fragile thread back to myself.

I didn't know what to expect from therapy. I had never done it before at least, not like this. The word psychologist felt clinical, but I was too broken to care what it was called. I just needed help. I needed someone who could see what I couldn't articulate.

Because of COVID, our sessions were on Zoom. I sat on the same couch I had barely moved from in weeks, the laptop balanced in front of me, camera angled awkwardly. I had a blanket wrapped around me like armor. My voice was shaky. My eyes felt swollen. But she didn't flinch.

She didn't press. She didn't ask me to explain everything all at once. She started gently, asking about my job. About what had happened. As the weeks progressed, almost seamlessly, she moved into questions about my family. My childhood.

I had a good childhood, I said. We had what we needed. There was no trauma.

She nodded gently, smiling. "Tell me more about your relationship with your parents."

I paused. And then, without thinking, I told her a story my mom used to tell with a laugh.

Our family car had just been painted. It was in the driveway drying.

My sister and I must've climbed up and played on it, leaving little footprints across the hood. We were in the bath when my father came home. He walked in, picked us up one at a time, spanked us, and walked out. My mom didn't even know what was happening. She said he just left her with two wet, screaming kids.

I waited for the therapist to laugh, too.

She didn't.

Instead, she looked at me, soft but serious. "That must've been terrifying." I blinked. I mean, I never thought of it that way. It's just a story. My mom always laughed about it.

She tilted her head. "Do you think it taught you anything? About safety? About what happens when you do something wrong?"

The question lingered and the space between my response. Maybe it did. Maybe that moment had etched itself in me. *Be good. Don't cause problems. Don't disappoint. Don't make Dad mad.* And from that experience, a way of being took root — one that would shape everything that followed. People-pleasing. Overachieving. Always anticipating everyone else's needs. Losing track of my own.

Later in one of our sessions, after I had shared yet another story of feeling obligated to help someone, of doing what I thought I "should," my therapist asked me, "Do you remember any sayings or beliefs that were ingrained in you as a child?" Without hesitation, I told her: "Put yourself in someone else's shoes."

It was something my mom used to say often and I took it to heart. Maybe a little too much. As a kid, I remember not just imagining how someone else felt, but fully absorbing it. I'd internalize their discomfort, their disappointment, their joy until I couldn't separate it from my own.

That tendency never really left me.

In adulthood, I'm often called "Switzerland." The neutral friend. The easy one. The one who doesn't cause waves. And if I do have a strong opinion, I almost always end up caving to avoid discomfort. Not because I don't care but because confrontation feels unbearable. It feels like a loss of connection, like rejection.

Around this time, I was deep into therapy, finally starting to unravel the patterns I had lived in for so long. I was learning about boundaries, people-pleasing, and how much of my life had been shaped around keeping others comfortable, even at the expense of myself.

That's when a close friend asked me to go interior camping with her again. We'd gone once before and, on the surface, it had been a good trip. Interior camping, or backcountry camping, paddling into your site by canoe, setting up camp, sleeping in a tent, cooking over a fire, cleaning, dealing with whatever weather comes, and repeating the cycle day after day. It's beautiful, but it's work.

The thought of hauling gear, battling the wind in the canoe, and waking up damp in a sleeping bag didn't excite me. It made me want to retreat into myself. It wasn't just that my body was tired, it was that my whole life had felt like one long paddle upstream. Always carrying the weight. Always pushing through. Always proving I could handle it.

I realized I was tired of always doing hard things.

I didn't want to earn my rest anymore. I just wanted to be. To feel peace without paddling through it first.

But I told her yes.

Not because I wanted to go but because she was excited, and I didn't want to disappoint her. She didn't have many people to camp with, and I didn't want her to feel alone. So I said yes and never even hinted that I didn't want to.

And then something strange happened, I started feeling irritated with her. Snapping in my mind. Avoiding her texts. Building this resentment that didn't make sense. She hadn't done anything wrong. But something in me was triggered.

So I brought it up in therapy.

"I don't get it," I told my therapist. "I said yes, but now I'm mad at her, and she didn't do anything."

She paused, then asked me, "Do you even like camping?"

"Of course I do," I said automatically.

She tilted her head. "Do you... really?"

"No," I whispered. "Not really. I don't like the work. I don't want to paddle, or cook over a fire, or wake up cold and wet. I want a cozy bed. A hot bath. I want ease."

And then came the shame.

Saying it out loud felt like confessing to a weakness. I had always equated women who camped with strength, independence, capability. Admitting that I didn't like it felt like admitting I wasn't enough.

But what my therapist helped me see was this: The anger I was feeling wasn't about my friend, it was about me. It was the frustration of constantly abandoning myself to keep others comfortable. Of ignoring my own needs, preferences, and energy to protect someone else's feelings. And that's what people-pleasing is, at its core, self-abandonment dressed as kindness. She challenged me to tell my friend the truth.

"What are you afraid will happen?" she asked.

And when I sat with it, the answer was clear.

"I'm afraid she won't like me anymore. That she'll think we have nothing in common. That she'll leave."

It was such a deeply rooted fear, I couldn't even bring myself to call my friend and tell her I didn't want to go. My body would stop me. Nausea, sweaty palms, racing heart. Every attempt ended in physical panic.

Eventually, my therapist offered another way. "Would you be willing to text her?" she asked. "Not something I normally suggest but maybe that's the first step."

Even that was hard. But I wrote the message. I hit send and immediately put my phone away. I couldn't even look at it.

Later, I picked it up with dread pooling in my stomach. I opened her reply expecting disappointment, but there was none.

She simply wrote, "Oh, I didn't know you didn't want to go. That's totally fine."

That was it.

The catastrophic outcome I'd been preparing for didn't happen. It never did. But my nervous system didn't know that yet. It had been wired to brace for rejection, for abandonment, for being "too much" or "not enough."

That moment changed something in me. I realized that I had been building stories in my head for years, stories where I was unloved if I spoke my truth, unworthy if I had preferences, unlikable if I disappointed anyone.

But therapy helped me begin asking: Do I want to do this? Do I like this?

It sounds simple. But for me, it was revolutionary. Because I started choosing me.

My therapist and I kept at it, week after week. She introduced the idea of inner child work. It was something I had never heard of, let alone considered for myself. "There's a younger version of you," she explained. "And she's still carrying a lot. Fear. Shame. Confusion. You can talk to her. You can listen to her. You can give her what she never got."

It sounded strange, even silly. But it also felt true.

I started noticing things I hadn't before. I started feeling my body, really feeling it. Noticing how tense and shaky I got when we talked about work. How heavy my chest got when she mentioned fear.

She'd often ask, "Where do you feel that in your body?"

At first, I didn't know. I said I didn't feel it anywhere. But the truth was, I felt it everywhere. I had always felt it, I just didn't know what it was. I didn't know it was my body screaming. It was a normal feeling for me.

Then one day, she asked a new question, "What brings you joy?"

I stared at her.

"I don't know."

"What do you do just for you?"

I fumbled. "I take care of my kids. Bring them to sports. Clean the house. Visit friends."

She smiled gently. "Okay, what's something you do that's just for Erin?"

I panicked.

"I run," I blurted out.

She nodded. "Do you love running?"

"Yes, of course." It was my automatic answer. But she asked again, with curiosity, not doubt.

"Do you love it, or do you love the identity of being someone who runs?"

The question hit like lightning. Sudden, sharp, and piercing.

If I'm being honest, and I was committed to honesty in therapy, no matter how uncomfortable or embarrassing it was to be so, I didn't love running. I wanted to love it. I wanted people to think I loved it. I wanted to be seen as strong, dedicated, fit. Runners were admired, and I craved that admiration.

I wanted the image not the experience.

And if that wasn't true joy then what else in my life wasn't real joy either? How many things had I done for how they made me look, not how they made me feel? Suddenly, I wasn't sure who I really was.

Session by session, I kept peeling back layers. Sometimes I cried. Sometimes I just stared. A lot of the time, I simply said, "I don't get it." Trauma, nervous system, somatic memory, it all felt like a new language. But she never rushed me.

"Just notice, be curious," she'd say. "What happens in your body when we talk about these things?"

And I began to see. The tightness in my chest when I talked about work. The pit in my stomach when I recalled something from child-hood. The way my voice stumbled and caught when I tried to say. "I need..."

I had been surviving for so long, I didn't realize that in this surviv-al-mode I was actually living in a constant state of hyper-vigilance. My body had become a map of unprocessed fear. At some point, she asked me to think of my earliest memory of fear. I couldn't.

Because I had always felt afraid, I just never called it that. I thought it was normal. I thought I was the problem for being so sensitive, so reactive, so easily overwhelmed.

But I was starting to see my body wasn't the problem. My body was wise. It had always known. I just hadn't known how to listen.

And with that awareness came a hard truth I had built my entire life around "yes." Yes, I'll do it. Yes, I can handle it. Yes, I'll stay late. Yes, I'll take care of everything. Yes, yes, yes…

I didn't know how to say no. I didn't even know what I liked. Or wanted. Or needed.

One day, in the middle of a session, I said it aloud without intending to, "I think I'm just existing."

It was like the truth had been waiting at the edge of my mouth, begging to be spoken. I wasn't living. I was existing. Performing. Pretending. Keeping everything moving on the outside, while quietly disappearing on the inside. And it scared me. But it also gave me a starting place. Because once you see it, you can't unsee it. And you can't rebuild until you recognize what's been lost.

IN
SEARCH
OF
MEANING

I first learned about the Buddhist classes from a friend who had been practicing for years. She told me how Buddhism had helped her through some of the hardest times after her marriage dissolved, giving her a sense of peace and perspective that nothing else had. I remember listening, intrigued but uncertain. I wasn't looking for a belief system, but I was desperate for something, anything, that could help me make sense of the storm I had been living in since going off work.

Coming out of the first-responders retreat, my mind had cracked open just enough to consider new ways of thinking. I wasn't the same person who had walked in. I had spent these last few months since leaving work over-identifying with my suffering, wrapping it around me like a cloak, not realizing how much I was contributing to my own pain.

The retreat forced me to see things differently. One of the doctors had spoken gently about Buddhism, just in passing, as part of a discussion about different healing modalities. I barely registered it at the time. But later, when my friend mentioned a Buddhist temple about an hour and a half away that had started offering online classes due to COVID, something inside me gave me a little nudge: Do it. And so, I did.

Every Thursday evening, I logged into Zoom for my class, *In Search of a Meaningful Life*. Even the title hooked me, because wasn't that exactly what I was doing? Searching for meaning in all the shattered pieces of my life?

The first thing I noticed was that we were allowed to turn our cameras off. I was relieved. I could listen, move around my house, even do the dishes while absorbing the teachings. I wasn't ready to sit still. Meditation was always the opening exercise, and I tried, I really did. But I found it agonizing. Less than a year after going off work, my nervous system still couldn't handle stillness. Sitting with myself, doing nothing, felt unbearable.

The teacher, a Buddhist nun, began that first class by asking a question that sat heavy in my chest: "What is the ultimate supreme goal?"

I had no idea how to answer. I had never even thought about it before. She asked us to consider whether we believed family and friends were the most important things in life. That seemed obvious, of course they were. Wasn't that what we were all raised to believe? But then she said something that stopped me cold. "With family and friends comes suffering."

I felt my whole body resist. What was she talking about? Family is love. Friendship is connection. But as she explained, I started to see what she meant.

"The people we love the most are often the source of our deepest pain. We hold on to them so tightly that when they disappoint us, when they leave, when they die, our suffering is unbearable."

I thought about my sister. My mother. The ache of missing them, the hole they left behind. I thought about my ex-husband, my friends, David. The tangled mess of love and loss and anger. I wasn't ready to accept what she was saying, but I couldn't ignore it either. It made me question whether I was too open, too willing to believe people would protect my heart the way I tried to protect theirs.

She asked, "What gives a day meaning? What gives a life meaning?"

Her words sent my mind racing. What *did* give a day meaning? What gave life meaning? I had never truly stopped to ask myself that before. In that moment, the answers that came to me were my boys, my job, my friendships, the people I helped, how good of a mother I was, how reliable I was as a friend, as a girlfriend. It was everything I did for others, all the ways I showed up, all the ways I made myself valuable to the people around me. That's what I believed gave my life meaning, because without those things, without the reflection of who I was in the eyes of others, I wasn't sure who I would be.

In Buddhism, meaning doesn't come from external things, not even relationships. It comes from cultivating a peaceful mind, developing compassion, and loving yourself. She challenged us to wake up every morning and ask: How can I be a bit more compassionate to myself today?

It felt like she was speaking another language. I had never considered myself in that way before—never paused to ask what *I* needed, let alone offered myself kindness. My entire life had been about others: anticipating their needs, keeping the peace, protecting them from disappointment. Turning that care inward felt selfish, almost wrong, like I was breaking some unspoken rule. I'd forget to even try, slipping back into old patterns without realizing it. Self-compassion wasn't just new—it was uncomfortable. It was something I had never been taught, and part of me wasn't sure I was allowed to learn.

Week after week, she spoke about the habits we all fall into, habits that trap us in our pain. She explained that the more we focus on our problems, the more depressed we become. The realization struck me, sharp and sudden. Because that was exactly what I had been doing. Replaying every awful thing that had happened at work. The conversations, the betrayals, the moments that shattered me. Over and over, I was keeping them alive in my mind, fueling the same anger and sadness I had felt the day they happened. I wasn't just remembering my suffering, I was recreating it. And for what? I couldn't change the past. I couldn't go back and undo any of it. She said something that I held onto tightly in those early weeks, "If there's no remedy for something, there is no reason to be unhappy about it."

At first, I rejected it. How could I not be unhappy about what had happened to me? About what had been done to me? But slowly, I started to see I had a choice. I could keep letting these thoughts dictate my emotions, or I could recognize them for what they were, just thoughts. I could feel them arise and decide not to let them control me. A thought I'd never considered before crept in. If I can choose my thoughts, maybe I can choose my life, too.

As the classes continued, she spoke about patience—not the kind I was used to, where you grit your teeth and tolerate something, but true patience, which meant welcoming whatever came with an open heart. Not resisting, not fighting. I had spent so many years trying to control my environment, convinced it was the only way to stay safe. Letting go of that grip, allowing in something I didn't want or like, felt almost impossible. The thought of not resisting made me uneasy, like I'd be inviting danger right to my doorstep.

The messages and teachings often had me thinking about my past. About my childhood, always being told to go do something whenever I was still. I had internalized that message so deeply that even as an adult, any moment of stillness felt wrong, like I was failing at something. The nun spoke about our society and distractions, about how we can't just be. We are taught, even at a young age, that stillness isn't productive. That we must always be doing, creating, producing something.

As she spoke, something inside me stirred, a vague, unspoken tension. I drew my knees to my chest, shifting in search of comfort, but all I could feel was the tension building within me. I can't just sit and do nothing. I would go crazy.

The thought surfaced before I could stop it, automatic and absolute. But why? Why did the idea of simply *being* make me so uncomfortable? Why couldn't I just sit and read a book or watch a movie without the gnawing sense that I should be doing something else? Even here, in this quiet space, surrounded by the steady presence of the Buddhist nun, my mind raced ahead, already seeking the next thing.

I wasn't sure where this unease came from, but I could feel its roots stretching backward into my childhood. A connection forming, faint but insistent. I had spent my whole life moving, achieving, overperforming, proving. But proving what, exactly? And to whom? The nun's voice gently broke through my thoughts:

"When you say, I am angry, you are identifying with anger. But anger is not who you are. You are experiencing anger. It is a feeling, not an identity."

I exhaled, feeling the weight of those words settle into my chest.

How many times had I said it? I am angry. I am broken. I am lost over these past few months. No wonder I had felt so trapped. If I was these things, then how could I ever be anything else? But what if they weren't who I was at all? What if they were just passing states, like waves rolling in and out? The thought unsettled me. If I wasn't those things, then who was I underneath it all? For the first time, I let the questions sit without rushing to fill the silence.

YOUNG
LOVE

The fire cracked in the old fireplace in the living room of a 16th-century Scottish castle where I sat on an antique velvet couch, surrounded by seven of the most extraordinary women I know. We had come to this place to mark a milestone birthday, to celebrate friendship, freedom, and the kind of hard-earned wisdom that only time and tears can gift you.

The room smelled of aged wood and centuries of peat smoke, and the windows behind us framed the soft, misty green of the Highlands. There was something sacred about it all — a stillness that seemed to hold centuries of stories in its walls. We had just returned from a day out exploring, bellies full of laughter and wine, still carrying stories on our lips as we tucked into thick-knit blankets and the kind of soul-deep comfort you can only find in the company of women who really see you.

I pulled out my phone to scroll through Instagram, something light, thoughtless. My youngest son, Oscar, had posted a story. It was a clip from the night before. He had gone to see his dad play live. Both being musicians, this was nothing out of the ordinary for them. The venue? A bar I used to work at when I was barely more than a girl. The song? That song. The one that was everywhere on the radio when I met his father. The one he had written with his band before I ever knew what it meant to fall in love, to fall apart, to fall into a life you build and then outgrow.

In the clip, I saw the man I used to love on stage. My ex-husband. The same man I had met more than thirty years ago. The same man who once made my heart thump so loudly I swore people could hear it. The same man was playing the song that once felt like a prophecy and now felt like a ghost. The same man was in the place where I used to spend every evening working over three decades ago. I felt my breath woosh from my chest.

And I fell apart.

Not loudly. Not with drama. But silently, completely. The tears came so fast I didn't know what hit me. My girlfriend beside me leaned in, her eyes wide with sudden concern.

"Oh my God, are you okay?"

I shook my head gently.

"I think so," I whispered, not really sure. "I don't know why I'm crying."

But I knew.

My heart remembered. My body remembered. It was doing what bodies do. It remembered being eighteen. It remembered falling in love.

We were driving south from my friend's cottage in her brand new car, windows down, the smell of pine and lakewater still clinging to our skin. And then the song came on the radio.

His band's song.

My whole body jolted.

"Oh my God, this is it!" I screamed, scrambling for the volume knob. The sound filled the car like midday sunlight. My friend and I belted the lyrics, singing so loud it felt like joy was pouring out of our pores. I couldn't believe it. He wrote this. He actually wrote this. The man I had just started dating. The man who kissed me like he already knew my secrets. The man who made my stomach flip every time he looked at me.

There was a wildness in me then, a sense of freedom. Like I had the whole world ahead of me. And maybe I did. I was in love, or at least whatever you call that feeling at eighteen when everything is new and glittering and unmarked by disappointment. I thought I had found it. Him. The one.

And he did feel like magic back then. He had a big smile and a soft voice and a band that people actually listened to. He was different from anyone I'd ever known. Older. Edgy. Messy. Mysterious. And he saw me. When I was with him, I felt wanted. Lit up. Real.

I can still see the way he looked at me back then, like I was the lyrics that were flowing out from him onto the page. Wondrous. Excited. In awe. His eyes had that way of softening right before he pulled me in, like he wanted to memorize the shape of me. We'd spend hours lying on his futon bed, wrapped up in each other, the world outside our cocoon irrelevant. We'd eat Kraft Dinner and stay up way too late, laughing until it hurt. I thought that was love. And maybe, in some way, it was.

There was something about the way he carried himself, unguarded, unpolished, that made me feel like I could exhale. Like I didn't have to be the good girl, the smart one, the perfect one. He didn't ask me to be anything other than who I was. But the thing is, I didn't really know who that was yet. I just knew I liked who I was when I was with him.

We told each other everything. From day one, it felt like we were in it for the long haul. He wanted to know my dreams, my fears, my wildest ideas for the future, and I wanted to hear his, too. We didn't have boundaries, or even a life outside each other. Our whole mission was to make one another happy. That kind of devotion felt like forever. And for a while, it was.

I began to pour myself into him. I became the kind of girlfriend who remembers the smallest things, who cheers loudest at shows, who runs to the bar after work just to catch the last song. I started weaving my worth into how well I could love him. How supportive. How present. How perfect. How I could be all these things for him.

He proposed to me on a beach in Los Angeles on Christmas Eve. It was warm, dreamy, cinematic. Everything about it was romantic and right. We were in our twenties, renting a tiny apartment beneath swaying palm trees. He'd wake up in the mornings grinning at the sunshine like it was made just for him.

He was easy-going. Almost nothing rattled him. And I was the opposite.

Tense. Overthinking. Always five steps ahead. Not because I wanted to be, but because I had to be. That was my survival. Stay sharp. Stay ready. Stay in control. He lived with his head in the clouds, sure everything would work out. I lived with one eye on the door, bracing for the next thing to crash through it.

We got married a year later in a little church in my hometown in Canada. I was just shy of twenty-one. Surrounded by friends and family, I was thrilled to become his wife. I wanted that title. I wanted to belong to someone who made me feel seen, even if I didn't yet know how to see myself.

Nothing really changed after marriage. We were still us, two dreamers, figuring it out together. Still living in L.A., still chasing something, together.

Looking back now, I realize how deeply my worth was tied to him and our marriage. To how he looked at me. To whether we were happy. To whether I was doing a good job being his wife. If he looked at me like he always did, then I was worthy of being looked at with love. If we were happy, then I was worthy of being happy. If I was a good wife, then I was worthy of being married to him. It wasn't the wedding that started me on this path or even our relationship, I had been abandoning myself and tying my worth to things outside myself long before then.

We had nine years together before kids—nine years of being each other's whole world. We didn't have much money, but it didn't matter. We were spontaneous—late-night drives, beach days with nothing but a blanket and a bottle of wine. We were best friends and co-conspirators, living like the world was ours to figure out.

When I got pregnant with Owen, it felt like life shifted into technicolor. My then husband was incredible during those months, attentive in ways I'd never known from anyone before. He'd rest his hand on my belly and talk to our baby like he was already part of the band. We'd go to his shows and laugh about how Owen would surely be born with a guitar in his hands.

When Owen arrived, we spent those first weeks wrapped up in each other, nestled in our bed with this tiny new person between us. Our hearts had never felt so full. By the time our second son Oscar came along, we felt complete. A family of four, two healthy boys, and a home back in Canada across the street from our best friends. It felt like the dream.

But somewhere in those early years, his career changed course, maybe stalled, maybe just lost its rhythm, and I'm not sure he ever found his footing again. Or maybe he never really had it to begin with, and I just didn't notice because we were too busy living in the rush of it all.

When our boys were born, my life changed in an instant. His didn't. He still played gigs late into the night, still slept in, still had adult conversations with friends over drinks. Yes, it was work, but it was also freedom, the space to breathe, to choose when to show up. My world had none of that.

Mine was small and relentless—diapers, feedings, appointments, and a hundred invisible tasks only I seemed to notice. I became the keeper of everything, the schedule, the bills, the groceries, the safety net. I worked too, but there was no awareness from him of the exhaustion that came with carrying it all. I didn't yet have the awareness to name it, to say out loud: *This is too much.* It just leaked out sideways, in sharp tones and quiet resentment I didn't want to admit to. Complaining felt like weakness, and I told myself other mothers had it harder.

Over time, I began noticing things I'd once brushed off and over-looked. The unpredictable income, the last-minute plans, the money choices that made my stomach clench. When we were young, those things had felt like part of the adventure. With kids, they felt like instability, and instability terrified me. He didn't want to change. He wanted to keep living the way he always had. And I couldn't. Not anymore. Stability for the kids, and for me, wasn't optional anymore.

It was no longer us against the world. It was him doing what he'd always done… and me quietly taking it all on. Over time, the "us" we had built started to fade. We stopped dreaming together. We stopped looking at each other like we were the best thing that had ever happened. I didn't feel chosen anymore, just expected.

There wasn't one big explosion, no single moment to point to. Just a slow, steady drip of loneliness until the bucket overflowed. By the end, I wasn't holding on to a marriage. I was holding on to my boys, my peace, and my sanity.

And when we finally separated, my biggest fear, being without him, turned into the clearest truth of all: I had been living without him for a long time. I had been doing it alone before he left. The only real difference now was that I no longer had to carry the weight of his unpredictable behavior along with everything else. In some ways, letting go was lighter than holding on.

INTERWOVEN

I was sitting in my cruiser, parked in the same quiet lot where I often caught up on notes and paperwork. The engine was idling, adding white noise in the background, but today my mind wasn't on work. I was gripping my phone so tightly my knuckles ached.

David and I had just come back from a trip to Mexico. We had a huge fight. I can't even remember what it was about now, only how it ended. His silence. That deliberate, punishing quiet I knew too well. It wasn't just uncomfortable, it scraped at something deep and old in me. That feeling of being shut out. Unworthy. Alone.

I had called my friend from the hotel in Mexico. She was one of my closest friends, one of the only people who really knew what was happening in my relationship. When the walls closed in, she was the person I reached for. My lifeline. The one I trusted to listen, to hold the layers of what I couldn't say anywhere else, to not judge me for staying even when things were breaking me apart.

But now, back home, back in uniform, and sitting in my cruiser, Mexico a memory, I was hearing something I couldn't fathom.

"I can't do this anymore, Erin," she said gently, but firmly. "I can't keep hearing these terrible things you're going through, only to have you tell me a day later that you two are fine again. And then I'm left... waiting for the next time. I need a break."

The words landed before I could make sense of them. My chest tightened, my throat burned, my eyes stung. I didn't argue. I didn't beg her to stay. I just sat there, silent, as she let go. As she let me go.

When the call ended, I stared at my phone like maybe she'd change her mind and call me back. But she didn't. The distance was deafening. I felt hollow. Lost. Like I'd been dropped in the middle of a road with no map, no one coming to find me. And under all of it, a heart-wrenching question: Why does this keep happening to me?

I didn't have the self-awareness then to see my part in it, the way I clung to her, pouring all of my pain into her without giving her any real way to help me. Without ever changing anything about my situation. I thought what I needed was for her to listen, to be my safe place. I didn't realize that I was asking her to carry something that just kept getting heavier. A weight that wasn't even hers to hold.

And in doing so, I pushed her away.

She wasn't the first friend I'd lost. That pattern went back much further.

I was seventeen when I met a friend who was about to start her first year of university, standing on the edge of adulthood the way I was too. We fell into friendship easily, like we had been waiting for each other. Both of us were restless, full of big feelings and bigger dreams, and in each other we found someone who understood. We became the kind of friends who shared everything, secrets, fears, visions of who we might become. We stayed up late on the phone, swapping stories until sleep finally won, her voice carrying me through some of my loneliest nights. She even came to visit me once I moved to L.A. Ours was the kind of friendship you believe will stretch across miles and years without faltering.

We were in each other's big moments—weddings, moves, celebrations. But it wasn't just that. We were woven into the ordinary days too, into the fabric of each other's lives in ways that felt like family. We laughed until our faces hurt. We grew up together in heartbreaks and hard choices. Those years stitched us into each other's stories.

And then, her father died.

It was sudden and it shattered her world. She was consumed with grief, with the tidal wave of pain that comes when the ground shifts under your feet and nothing feels safe anymore. I wanted to be there for her. But I was in LA, staying with a friend who rented a room in someone else's home. This was the late '90s—no cell phones, no FaceTime, no way to connect instantly. The only phone belonged to the owner of the house. It wasn't ours, it was meant for local calls and incoming ones, not long-distance.

When my husband called and told me the news, the floor fell out beneath me. I was devastated for her. I remember thinking how grateful I was that she must have been surrounded by her husband, her family, the people who loved her most. And I was thousands of miles away, helpless. In my heart, I told myself she would know that once I was home, I'd show up. That I'd be there in whatever way I could.

But I didn't understand grief then. I hadn't lost anyone I loved yet, so I didn't know what it demanded. I didn't know how much presence matters, or that sometimes a gesture, flowers, a card, speaks louder than words. In my inexperience, I thought a phone call when I returned would be enough.

When I finally got home, I left her a message. But for her, it wasn't enough. I hadn't sent flowers. I hadn't reached across the gap in the way she needed. I didn't even realize I was supposed to. Not because I didn't care, but because I was young, naive, and utterly unequipped to meet her in that kind of pain.

Her message back to me was sharp with hurt. And I took it as final, that our years-long friendship was over. I told myself I had failed her beyond repair, that I was a terrible friend, that the bridge had burned and there was nothing I could do. I didn't fight for it. I didn't ask her what she needed. I didn't tell her I was sorry. I just… let it end.

We lost seven years of each other's lives.

She missed the births of my sons. The unraveling of my marriage. So many moments that mattered and the ones that didn't. And I missed hers. Entire chapters of our lives were erased from each other's stories because I didn't know how to hold conflict. Because I thought retreating into silence was safer than showing up clumsy but honestly.

Years later, out of nowhere, she reached out through my dad. She asked him for my number. One afternoon, the phone rang, and when I picked up, it was her voice on the other end. Seven years had passed, but it was still warm. Familiar. She told me she had missed me. Slow road back together began.

When I look back at that situation, I can see it wasn't about not caring, it was about not knowing how. I didn't have the tools for honest conflict or repair. I didn't know how to have those hard conversations meant to repair. I thought her disappointment meant I was unworthy, that I had failed beyond redemption. So instead of leaning in, I shut down.

That falling out taught me something I carry even now. Silence might feel safe in the moment, but it can cost you the people you love most.

By the time that first friendship began to repair, I was already years into another one. This one wasn't new or fragile, it was rooted. We were, like my other friend, deeply woven into the fabric of each other's lives.

We met while flying, and from the very beginning, it felt like we just understood each other. Our friendship blossomed quickly, and it wasn't long before our families blended too. She and her husband became like an aunt and uncle to my boys, steady and loving presences during those early years of motherhood. Their kids were older, but my boys adored them, even looked up to them. They babysat, they played, they became the first friends my boys ever knew.

Even our husbands clicked, though they couldn't have been more different. Her husband once joked, "We have enough friends," when she first mentioned me, but somehow, we slipped in anyway. They welcomed us into their lives wholeheartedly. It meant more than I could ever put into words.

We were so close that when the elderly woman across the street from them was preparing to sell her house, we planned for us to buy it. It seemed like the most natural thing in the world, raising our families just steps apart, sharing driveway chats, impromptu dinners, and everyday life together. It wasn't just friendship. It was family. Our chosen family.

And then when my marriage began to fracture, I leaned on them. Hard.

I was hurting, angry, coming undone in ways I had no way to process. Motherhood felt heavy, my needs went unmet, my marriage was slipping through my fingers. And I didn't hide it. With them, I let it all spill out. The disappointment. The frustration. The pieces of my life I was barely holding together.

From the outside, I'm sure it looked messy. Irrational. Maybe even unhinged at times. My husband, always calm and easygoing, made my pain look exaggerated. He played the part of the patient one—the charming one, the good guy. And that only deepened my shame, because inside, I was coming apart in more ways than one. His silence, his steadiness, his ability to seem unbothered, left me spiraling harder. And they saw all of it.

When my husband and I finally separated, I thought our friends would still be mine. That they'd hold space for me, for the boys, for the new reality I was thrust into. What I didn't expect, what left me reeling, was how quickly the tide turned. He told his version of the story. The polished one. The one where he was the good guy. And that was the story they held. Maybe not because they truly believed it, but because he was so skilled at playing the victim that it felt easier to accept his version than to question it.

I didn't challenge it. I didn't defend myself. I didn't lean into the discomfort with conversation or clarity or even fighting it. I did what I had always done when I sensed disappointment. I went silent.

And in what felt like a blink, they were gone from my life.

Not just her. Not just their kids. But the family I had built my life around. My village. My safe place.

I stayed in the house for a while, but the silence from across the street was unbearable. I'd watch from my window as he pulled into their driveway, my boys tumbling out of the car to be greeted with open arms.. They'd have dinner, spend hours together, and I'd sit alone, grieving. Not just the end of my marriage, but the end of belonging.

Eventually, I sold the house. To them, actually. The entire transaction happened without a single conversation between her and me. It was handled through her husband.

The boys and I moved away, and with that move, an entire era of my life ended.

It wasn't just the loss of friendship. The milestones we'd never celebrate together, the laughter and conversations at the backyard BBQ, the future we once imagined living across the street from each other, all of it evaporated overnight. I grieved it deeply. I carried that loss with me for years.

I can see my part in it now. I leaned too hard. I poured my pain out without boundaries, without giving her room to breathe. I asked her, and them, to endure more of me than anyone could. But at the time, all I could feel was the hollow ache of being left behind.

That loss marked me. It left a scar so deep that for years every friendship I had was shadowed by the fear that it could end just as suddenly. If I was too much, or not enough, they'd leave. And because I didn't know how to hold my own pain, I handed it to the women closest to me. I clung too tightly. I poured too much. I leaned so hard they couldn't breathe.

I see it now, I wasn't just anxiously attached to my romantic partners, I was anxiously attached to my friends. I didn't have many, usually just one or two who carried my whole heart. And when those bonds cracked, I broke with them.

The wisdom I hold now is that those friendships didn't fall apart because I was unworthy, it was because I didn't yet know how to be interwoven with someone else. I didn't know how to sit with my own hurt before sharing it. I didn't know how to ask for what I needed without shame. I didn't know how to be my own anchor.

Life, in its relentless way, taught me how to stand on my own and have people close to me.

And maybe the most beautiful part of this story is that all three of these women are in my life today. Despite the tears, the silences, the heartbreak, we found our way back. Not in the same way as before, but softer, wiser, truer. Proof that some bonds are meant to last.

Today, I no longer hand one person my whole world. I have circles of women now. Communities. Sisters. They remind me of who I am, they lift me when I fall, and they sit beside me when life is heavy. They are my chosen family.

Through it all, I've learned to be a friend to myself. To love myself more than I need others to love me. To be my own steady ground.

MOTHER'S DAY

The server sets down another mimosa, and I laugh at something Oscar says. Owen is already in the middle of a story, his hands flying in the air the way they do when he's excited. The table is crowded with food, pancakes stacked high, eggs still steaming, fruit tumbling from bowls. It looks like every Mother's Day table should, messy, abundant, threaded with laughter.

But inside me, there's a twinge of longing sitting right at the bottom of my heart.

Because while I am a mother, I don't have a mother. And on this day, that absence is everywhere.

It's there when the hostess led us past tables of three generations, grandmother, mother, daughter, their laughter rising over coffee cups, a lineage intact.

It's in the aisles of grocery stores, cards lined up with words I'll never get to write: Thanks for always being there. I couldn't have done it without you.

It's in the quiet of my phone, the silence of the conversations we never had.

Mother's Day reminds me that I didn't lose her all at once. I lost her slowly, to a disease that took her piece by piece, until one day, she was just... gone.

I was ten when my mom was diagnosed with multiple sclerosis. She was only thirty-three. Back then, there wasn't much information. No real explanations, just uncertainty. Fear moved into our house and never left.

As the disease took hold, her world narrowed to the work of surviving it. Survival demanded so much of her that there simply wasn't enough left for the small, ordinary things a daughter needs.

By the time I had children, she was living in a nursing home, present in form but largely absent in everything I wanted from a mother.

When Owen was born, a nurse wheeled me into my room, every step of the day leaving me bone-tired and oddly exposed. I held this tiny new life to my chest and looked across the hall, where another new mother sat propped on pillows, hair damp and face both exhausted and luminous. An older woman hovered beside her, knowing exactly how to fix a blanket, how to hold water, how to provide what wasn't even asked for. The young woman murmured, "Mom, can you get me a coffee?" The older woman bustled out into the corridor, returning minutes later with a steaming cup, a small bouquet, and a stuffed toy for the baby. I looked back down at Owen and felt the absence of my own mother like a hand on my shoulder.

I looked around my own room. It was just me, Owen bundled against my chest, and my husband slouched in the chair by the window. No mom bustling in with coffee. No mom leaning over to kiss my forehead. No mom to tell me I was doing okay. Her absence felt more overwhelming than the physical pain of childbirth.

Years later, the same absence showed up again, quieter, but just as sharp. It was four in the morning when I woke to the weight of Oscar's little body curled against mine. His breath was warm on my arm, sleeping soundly and safely in a way that made my own chest ache. I reached over, half-asleep, expecting to find my husband beside me, but his side of the bed was cold. Empty.

He should have been home hours ago.

I slipped out of bed carefully so I wouldn't wake Oscar and quietly snuck into the living room. The house was quiet in that hollow way that amplifies every thought. The clock on the wall glowed red: 4:07.

I sank down against the wall, knees pulled to my chest, and the tears came before I could stop them. I was wrung out, angry, scared—every small thing felt too much to handle alone. More than anything I wanted my mom. I imagined stuffing the boys' pajamas and stuffed animals into a bag, piling them into the car, and driving to her house just to crawl into her bed until the world felt safe again

But there was no house to go to. No mom waiting up. Just me, in the dark, trying to figure out how to survive alone.

That's what it's like to not have a mom. Every rough patch, every heartbreak, every moment where I just wanted to feel held, I had nowhere to go. No soft landing place. No unconditional love waiting simply because I was hers. The absence isn't loud, it doesn't shout. It shows up in the softest places, in the middle of the night, in the ache of an empty bed, in the longing for a place that never existed.

Years later, when I stood at the top of a dock, moments away from walking toward David to become his wife, another wave of that absence hit me. The chapel floated over the water, the glass glinting in the sun. It was the kind of romantic setting little girls dream about. My dress rustled softly as I stood waiting for the music to start. And she wasn't there to see it.

My mom wasn't there. She would never be there again.

It's not just the milestones. It's the everyday moments, the ones most people take for granted.

I'll never call my mom while stirring pasta to ask what she used to make for dinner on the nights we needed something warm and familiar. I'll never stand beside her in a department store, holding up dresses and asking which one looks better. I'll never lean on her when my body changes with age, asking what it felt like for her, what to expect, how to survive it.

I watch my friends with their mothers—the way they bicker like sisters in the mall, the way their phone calls stretch for an hour about nothing, the way they book girls' weekends together. That easy shift from mothering into friendship, that companionship that comes in adulthood. I have longed for it my whole life.

Every May, the ache sharpens. No matter the years that pass, it never dulls.

My boys, though, have never failed to make Mother's Day special. From burnt toast carried in on a tray when they were small, to brunches like this one now, their laughter filling every empty space. I love it. I treasure it.

But Mother's Day is always bittersweet. Because I am a mother without a mother. And on this day, more than any other, I carry both truths, the love I've been given, and the love I'll always miss.

RAY

I always got nervous when I didn't hear from Ray for a few days.

My mind would start to spiral, what if this is it? What if today is the day he dies? I'd tell myself I was overthinking, that maybe he was just resting or with his family. But my body always carried the fear. And that day, it felt different. It was as if the air shifted inside me, thick and hard to swallow — a signal my body recognized before my head did. There was always a quiet fear living in me when it came to Ray, but this time it pressed harder, more certain.

So when his text came through, I froze. We'd been messaging almost daily ever since he went off work on sick leave, the leave that turned permanent because he was dying. And there wasn't a damn thing I could do about it. I stared at my screen, bracing myself. This felt like the one.

It started gently, loving. Ray never started a message or conversation like that. He'd usually jump right in, like we'd just hit unpause on the same conversation we'd been having for years. No prelude, no small talk just right into it. That's why this one felt different.

"Your friendship has meant more to me than anything in this world."

I felt the blood drain from my face. My breath caught. My throat closed. My ears felt pressurized.

"You changed my life. You brought joy back to a place where there had been sadness for so long. You made me believe I could love again. And for that, I'll always be grateful."

My hands trembled. I could hear his voice in my mind as I read, calm and steady. Familiar. God, so familiar.

"Would things have been different if we lived closer? Maybe. Who knows. But the love and support you've given me over these past six years... they've been the best of my life."

I was crying by then. Hot, breathless, gut-wrenching sobs.

"Even though we lived far apart, we made each other a priority. You made me feel special. You made me feel loved again. I couldn't have gotten through this without you."

"I'll try to message again. But the doctors... they're saying it won't be long now. I'll make sure someone contacts you if I can't. Just know I love you, keep living, keep loving, and don't waste the life you have."

That was the last message. I never heard from him again.

He was dying. And I wasn't there. I couldn't be there. And no one really knew what we were to each other, what he was to me.

There was no funeral for me to attend, not really. His wife, who he loved deeply, didn't know the whole story. How could she? Ray and I never told our partners just how close we were to each other, or that we spoke nearly every day. Not because we were hiding something, but because there was no simple way to explain it. Our friendship was deep, rare, the kind of bond that could easily be misunderstood. We didn't want our significant others to feel threatened, or worse—force us to choose.

Because what Ray and I shared wasn't something that fit into a tidy box.

It wasn't romantic. But it was love. Deep, unwavering love.

An old love. Rooted in the way someone can just... know you. Because he did. He knew me. The real me. And I knew him.

We didn't become friends as adults. We became friends decades before, when I was twelve years old, standing barefoot on a sandy beach in the small town I lived in.

I met Ray the summer I turned twelve. It was at the day camp my sister Robyn and I went to every year. By then, I had already earned all the swimming badges the camp offered, so during swim time, I was just sitting on the beach, legs tucked up to my chest, watching the other kids splash through their groups.

That's where Ray found me. He was sixteen, tall, confident, and tan from a summer of lifeguarding. I remember him walking over, water still dripping from his hair, looking right at me with kind eyes and asking: "Hey, what group are you in?"

"I'm not in one," I said, probably a little shy. "I already passed all my badges."

He smiled. "Wanna help me teach mine?"

That's how it started. I think he was teaching blue badge at the time, though that detail fades behind the memory of how he made me feel seen, included, invited in. I said yes before he could change his mind.

From that day forward, every swim session, I was by his side, helping him with the younger kids, feeling special just to be near him.

Ray also taught classes down at the town dock, and I'd conveniently wander down there more than I needed to, lingering at the edge of the water and pretending I had some other reason to be there. The truth was simple: I couldn't take my eyes off him. At twelve, every glance, every half-smile felt like the biggest thing in the world.

But Ray never made me feel silly. He wasn't flirtatious or dismissive. He was kind. Gentle. Protective. In hindsight, I think he saw me the way an older brother might, a sweet kid who just wanted to be noticed. And he let me feel that I mattered.

Ray had three sisters. I didn't know that at the time, but it made sense. He had a natural way with girls, patient, respectful, easygoing. He was safe. And that summer, I had the kind of crush only a twelve year old can have on a sixteen year old boy. I adored him, completely and hopelessly, in the only way I knew how.

A traveling wrestling event was coming to town, a big deal in a tiny northern Canadian community like ours. One day at camp, Ray casually asked, "Hey, are you going to the wrestling show this weekend?" Of course I said yes. I had no idea it was even happening until that moment, but if Ray was going, I was going.

I ran home and told my mom, full of urgency. "There's a wrestling show at the arena and I have to go." She looked at me like I had three heads. "Wrestling? Since when do you like wrestling?"

I didn't. But I liked Ray.

Robyn and I went, and Ray met us there. He sat with us, made sure we were comfortable, and even took pictures with us. I still have a photo of him from that night. Ray, me, and a comically short wrestler grinning for the camera.

It felt like magic.

But like all summer things, it ended. Ray didn't live in my small town. He lived in a city two days drive away. And this was long before texting or Instagram or DMs. I remember hoping maybe, just maybe, he'd become my pen pal. We exchanged addresses. I think he wrote me once. But he was sixteen, and I was twelve, and the world moved on.

Still, that summer stayed with me.

The way he looked at me.

The way he listened to me.

The way I felt seen.

How I felt safe with him.

That kind of imprint doesn't fade.

It plants a seed you don't realize is still there, until one day, something makes it bloom.

It had been decades since I'd seen or spoken to Ray. Life had moved on. I'd become a mother. Married. Then separated. I was in the thick of my divorce, lonely, exhausted, and quietly trying to piece myself back together. It was one of those evenings when everything felt heavy, just too much. The boys were asleep, the house was quiet, and I was mindlessly looking through my Facebook feed.

I don't know what made me click into the day camp group for people who had attended that same little camp so many years ago.

Someone had posted: "What's your favorite memory from camp?" Thoughts of that summer flickered through my mind. The carefree feeling of being twelve again. Sitting on the beach. Laughing at the wrestling arena. Heart pounding when Ray walked by. Ray.

I kept reading through the comments, all these snippets of childhood joy and freedom. I felt like I was there again, barefoot, sun-kissed, and full of uncomplicated dreams. It was warm and nostalgic, and at the same time, bittersweet. I was in the middle of so much pain, trying to navigate separation, parenting, and self-doubt and reading those memories made me ache for something that felt so very far away—safety.

So I wrote a comment.

"Some of my best memories are from this camp. My sister and I went every year when we lived up north, and we absolutely loved it. I remember having the biggest crush on the swim instructor, Ray. I wonder where he is now!"

I posted it and forgot about it. Life pulled me back in. Making lunches. Folding laundry. Healing in slow motion.

Days, or maybe weeks later, I checked back. There were comments. And then I saw it.

Ray...

Ray!

His name. His face. His comment.

"Erin! Who knew?!"

I nearly dropped the coffee I was holding. I never expected him to see it, let alone respond. And there it was, there he was, all these years later, cutting through time like it had just been yesterday that we'd stood on the sand together.

My heart leapt and broke at the same time.

He messaged me privately soon after. Light-hearted and teasing, asking how I'd been, what I'd been up to. Laughing about my crush. We both had so much to say. So much life between us. Twenty years of stories, grief, love, disappointment, laughter, and somehow, we picked up as if the years between us hadn't happened.

At the time, he was going through a difficult divorce. So was I. We found each other right when we needed someone the most.

We messaged constantly after that. First on Facebook, then by text. Light at first, "Where do you live now?" "What have you been up to?" But soon, the conversations grew deeper, more vulnerable.

We were both navigating the aftermath of marriages that had crumbled. Both trying to make sense of who we were outside of being a partner, a parent, a provider. The timing was uncanny. We had each walked through our own hell, and here we were, meeting again as adults, quietly reaching for comfort in each other's words.

Ray was a few steps ahead of me in his divorce, which helped. I was still raw, still unsure of what came next. He listened. He answered questions I didn't want to ask my lawyer. And more than that, he just got it. The loneliness. The guilt. The identity unraveling. We were each other's sounding board, each other's truth.

And then one day, he messaged: "I'm coming to town for work. Want to meet for dinner?"

I was over the moon. I remember trying to rearrange everything. My sister Robyn was visiting with my niece, and I didn't want to leave them, but when I told her Ray had reached out and wanted to meet, she didn't hesitate. "Go," she said. "Go see him. I'll watch the boys."

So I did.

He was staying near the airport, and I drove out to meet him. I remember walking into the restaurant, spotting him across the room, and feeling like no time had passed at all. That warm energy. That easy smile. The way he stood up to hug me like we'd done this a thousand times as kids.

We talked for hours. First at the table, then at the bar once the restaurant transitioned into more of a nightlife scene. The music got louder, drinks were flowing, and we ended up dancing, laughing, completely wrapped in the comfort of each other's company.

For a moment, it felt like being kids again, like we'd slipped into an alternate universe where heartbreak didn't exist and time was a lie.

By the end of the night, we were both too tipsy to drive. He joked about me staying at his hotel, teasing, light-hearted. But then he did what most men hadn't done in my experience, he called a cab, walked me outside, and made sure I got home safe.

We talked about it later, laughing at how close it had felt, how easy it would've been to let the moment become something else. But Ray, being Ray, said, "It would've been a mistake. And it would've changed everything. I couldn't risk losing what we had."

And I respected him for it. Loved him for it.

Because maybe he was the first man in my life who didn't see me as a body first. Who didn't try to take. Who just wanted to know me. And be known.

From that night forward, we talked constantly. On the phone, in the car. Through every messy twist and turn of life. Morning commutes became our ritual, coffee in hand, Bluetooth on, baring our souls before the day had a chance to wear us down. It didn't matter where he was. He could be two provinces away and still make me feel like I wasn't alone in the world.

Ray was home and I felt safe again.

Ray didn't just support me, he believed in me. When I told him I was thinking about applying to become a police officer, he didn't hesitate. He didn't ask why. He didn't doubt me. He just said, "Hell yes! Do it."

I didn't know many women in policing back then, especially not single moms trying to start over. I wasn't sure if I'd make it, or if I was even allowed to dream of something bigger. But Ray could see it. He had this way of speaking the version of me I hadn't stepped into yet.

"You're going to be amazing at it. You don't see it yet, but I do."

And he didn't stop there. Ray had a friend in policing not far from where I lived, and he arranged my very first ride-along with him. That night, something in me clicked. I watched the way the officers moved, the weight of the job, the pace, the energy. I could actually see myself in the uniform. It wasn't just a fantasy anymore. It was possible.

I still remember walking back to my car after that ride-along, full of adrenaline and certainty. I called Ray immediately.

"I loved it," I told him. "I think I could really do this."

"I already knew that," he said.

We celebrated that moment like I'd already made it. Like the rest was just a formality.

But it wasn't easy. The application process was long and grueling. I had two little boys. I was still rebuilding my life. There were road-blocks and rejection letters and moments where I felt like I'd made a mistake, like maybe I was chasing something that wasn't meant for me.

I'll never forget the first time I got a rejection letter. I called Ray sobbing. I had poured everything into that application. And all it said was thanks, but no thanks. It gutted me.

Ray didn't sugarcoat it. He didn't tell me it was okay to give up.

"You're not done," he said. "Don't let them say no. Make them say yes."

He reminded me that timing wasn't always in our control, but persistence was. He reminded me that I had more power than I was giving myself credit for.

A year later, I applied again. By then, the boys and I were living with my dad. Life still wasn't easy, but I had grown thicker skin. I'd done the work. I was hopeful, but guarded.

I got the envelope on a weekday morning, plain, official-looking, the kind that makes waver between hesitancy and hope. I called Ray as I drove to work, envelope sitting in the passenger seat.

"It's here," I said.

"Well, what are you waiting for? Open it."

"I'm scared."

"Of what?"

"That it's another no."

"It's not."

With his voice in my ear, I pulled over. My hands were shaking. I opened the envelope and read the first line.

"Congratulations..." I broke down crying.

Ray started shouting on the other end of the line, screaming with joy. Cheering for me like I'd won the Olympics.

"I told you! I told you, Erin!"

That moment? That joy? That deep knowing that someone was proud of me? It lives in my bones. No matter how the career unfolded, that was the moment I became a police officer. Because someone I trusted looked at me and said: You belong here.

My first few years with David were confusing, painful, and incredibly lonely. From the outside, things probably looked stable. A new relationship. A fresh start. But inside, I was coming undone. I didn't understand what was happening, why I felt like I was walking on eggshells, second-guessing myself, shrinking.

I'd call Ray in tears. Sometimes I couldn't even explain why I was crying, I just knew that I didn't feel okay, and I didn't feel safe. There was a heaviness in my chest that never fully left. Ray didn't always know what to say. Sometimes he was quiet, other times he was angry at how I was being treated, but he never judged me. Never tried to fix me. He just stayed.

"You don't deserve this," he'd say gently. "But you're not broken. You're just scared."

He saw things I wasn't ready to see. My need to be loved. My desperation to hold on. The way I mistook crumbs for connection. He never pushed me, but he didn't let me lie to myself either.

Ray never made it about sides. He didn't slam David or turn me into a victim. He just kept pointing me back to myself, to what I deserved, to what I already knew in my gut.

He'd say, "I know you're scared. But the version of you that I know? She's in there. And she's strong as hell."

Ray taught me that love, real love, doesn't always come in romantic form. Sometimes, it comes in the shape of a friend who refuses to let you go numb. Someone who doesn't need anything from you except your truth.

He was my lighthouse in a time when I didn't even realize I was drowning. We never needed to label it. There was no jealousy. No agenda. We had tried, briefly, to explore the romantic possibility, asking each other and ourselves if we could make it work. But the distance, the timing, the mess of our lives… it just didn't align. So instead, we made a conscious decision.

"Let's just love each other, without expectation."

Not the kind of love that fades or flickers.

The kind that stays.

The kind you can call at the first blush of dawn or at midnight, to say nothing and still feel understood.

Ray taught me what emotional intimacy really is. And in doing so, he helped me learn to stop settling for less.

We met for breakfast one morning while he was in town. He didn't come into town often, so getting to see him in person felt like a gift. Sitting across from him with coffee between us, it felt wonderful just to be there, to see his face, to hear his laugh without a phone in between.

But I wasn't prepared for what he was about to tell me.

"I've been having some trouble with reflux," he said casually. "I'm going to get it checked out."

I remember tilting my head and asking if he thought it was anything serious. He didn't. Neither did I, at first. I figured they'd give him something for acid, maybe suggest a change in diet.

At the time, his girlfriend was going through breast cancer treatments. And he was showing up for her in the most beautiful, selfless way—loving, present, strong. So when he started having his own symptoms, I told myself it was probably stress. Too much on his plate. Nothing more.

But it was more.

Ray called me after his appointment. His voice was quieter than usual.

"It's cancer. Esophageal."

I didn't understand at first. It didn't register. You hear "esophagus" and you don't immediately realize how dangerous it is. But then I looked it up. And I panicked.

He told me the doctors were hopeful. There was a plan: chemo, radiation, rounds of treatment. He'd have to take a leave from his sales job. He was upset about that, but trying to stay positive. So I matched his energy. I said all the things I thought he needed to hear.

"You've got this."

"You're strong."

"You're going to beat it."

And for a while, he did.

I remember when he called me with the results, how well his body was responding to treatment. I was so relieved. His girlfriend was improving too. It felt like the universe was finally giving them both a break. After everything they had been through, they deserved healing. They deserved peace.

He even went back to work. Things felt almost normal again.

But then he called one day and said the symptoms were coming back. That familiar discomfort. That niggle of something returning. He didn't sound panicked. But I could feel it, the fear underneath the surface. I tried to reassure him again.

"It's probably nothing. Just scar tissue, right? You're fine. It's going to be fine."

But this time... it wasn't. The cancer was back. And it was aggressive. And there it was again, that old question I hated: Why does this keep happening to the people I love? First my mom. Then my grandmother. Now Ray.

I remember sitting on the edge of my bed, phone pressed to my ear, trying to hold it together while he explained the new prognosis. There weren't many options. It was terminal.

I couldn't breathe.

"You have to fight," I told him. "You beat it once. You can beat it again."

And he tried. He did. Ray fought like hell. He didn't go quietly. But it didn't matter. His body was tired. The cancer didn't care how good, how kind, how needed he was.

As his health declined he couldn't talk on the phone anymore. Speaking was too painful. Neither of us knew the last time we spoke to each other would be the last time we'd hear each other's voice. The heartache in that alone was debilitating. His voice was always my safe place. It was the place where with just one word I could be bursting into tears or laughing so hard my stomach ached. But he was still here, we still had each other. We moved to messages instead of phone calls. His strength was diminishing along with his health and his messages became less frequent. They became quiet in tone. The effervescence of his spirit wasn't there anymore.

In the final weeks, he still found ways to reach me, through short messages, usually late at night or early in the morning. Sometimes just a few words. But every message felt like a miracle. A treasure.

And then the last message came. No preamble, no small talk—just truth. He told me I had mattered. That I had made a difference. That he was grateful.

And then the final line, the one that still echoes in me: *"I love you. Keep living, keep loving, and don't waste the life you have."*

That was the end of our conversations. His final gift.

He was my best friend. My person.

But I wasn't his widow. I wasn't his wife.

We had no label for what we were.

I watched for updates on social media.

I read his death announcement from a Facebook post.

And I cried harder than I've cried in years.

Grief is strange when the world doesn't know what you've lost. There were no casseroles. No sympathy cards. No one asking how I was holding up. But inside, I was gutted. Hollow. Ray had been my constant through some of the hardest years of my life. He had held space for me when I didn't even know how to hold it for myself.

And then he was gone. No closure. No final hug. No chance to say, "Thank you for saving me."

Ray was never mine in a romantic sense. But he loved me more honestly than anyone ever had. No performance. No game. No possession. Just presence. Just truth. He showed me what it meant to love without strings. He taught me that emotional intimacy is love. That being known is the most sacred thing we can offer another human being.

There were no masks with Ray. No pretending. I could show up crying, confused, broken, and he never pulled away. And when the world fell out beneath him, he still found a way to check in on me. That's who he was. And that's who he'll always be.

His voice still echoes in my mind when I doubt myself:

"You've got this, Erin. Don't let them say no."

Ray's love was the purest kind—steady, unconditional, and without demand. Maybe he came into my life at that time to show me what real love could feel like. Not the kind built on needing to be chosen, but the kind that simply stays. It took years for me to truly understand the gift he gave me.

A year or so after he died, he came to me in a dream, one of those sacred in-between states where you're not quite asleep, not quite awake. I saw him. Felt him. His presence wrapped around me like it always had. I gasped with joy, "Oh my god, thank God, I thought you were dead." He looked at me with that same steady calm and said, "I am, Erin."

But the love between us hadn't gone anywhere. It pulsed through the air like light. When I woke, the feeling lingered, warm, familiar, real. I believe he came to check on me that night, the way he always did.

And I've carried that moment ever since. Because some loves don't leave. They become part of who you are.

ROBYN WITH A Y

Only close family and a few friends were there that day. It was October 22nd, 2020, a cool, overcast fall morning. The kind of day where the sky hangs low and the wind barely stirs, as if even nature knows something sacred is unfolding.

We gathered quietly, feeling the quiet ache of goodbye settle into every corner of the house. She had made the decision to take this final step in the comfort of her own home, surrounded by the people she loved, not in a sterile hospital room or unfamiliar space. That choice was so her, intentional, grounded in love, and deeply personal.

So we gathered there that morning, quietly honoring her wish to say goodbye on her own terms, in the place that held her life, her laughter, and her story.

It was a day of impossible courage. A day stitched together with heartbreak and grace. And while I'll never forget the pain of it, I carry something else too, the sacredness of that goodbye. The beauty in choosing to meet death with open eyes, and the unbearable privilege of walking beside someone you love as far as you can go.

I didn't know it would hurt this much.

Not because I didn't love her. I did. Fiercely. But I thought I had already grieved so much of her over the years I didn't know I had this much left in me. Watching someone you love disappear slowly into chronic illness is a kind of mourning all on its own. So when she told me she had chosen Medical Assistance in Dying, I understood.

I really did. But nothing could prepare me for what it felt like when she was actually gone.

Her name was Robyn with a Y, as she always made sure to tell people when we were young. She was my sister, born exactly twelve months to the day after me. For a while, we were raised like twins, inseparable, giggling, sharing secrets, fighting over clothes, finishing each other's sentences. We were "the girls." The Gorrie girls. And in many ways, we were each other's first best friend.

She was diagnosed with multiple sclerosis when she was just twenty years old. I watched the disease steal pieces of her slowly, like sand slipping through fingers, not all at once, but enough that every year felt heavier than the last. Years later, she was also diagnosed with scoliosis. Together, the two became a nightmare her body couldn't escape. The pain was relentless. Her independence dwindled. Life became small and predictable. "Groundhog Day," she used to call it. Wake up. Pain. Eat. Exist. Repeat.

But before all of that, there was the two of us.

Some of my favorite memories with Robyn are from the years we lived way up north. We were both athletic, all legs and big feet, slightly awkward but always moving. People used to laugh and say we hadn't grown into our bodies yet, which was probably true. I can still see us in our figure skating dresses, legs like little stilts, skates that looked too big, giggling through practices.

We were competitive figure skaters. In the winters, we practically lived at the rink. Early mornings before school meant patchwork— slow, intentional patterns traced into the ice, edge after edge, inside, outside, backwards, forwards. It was quiet, focused, cold, and beautiful. Our school was across the street from the arena, which made the transition from ice skates to school books easier and often came with a stop at the candy store with the red door. We'd sneak in with a few coins, grab a treat, and eat it in the playground, thrilled by the rebellion.

Summers were for bikes. We'd ride all across town, population five thousand, there were only two roads we weren't allowed on, Third Avenue and Main Street. We thought we had total freedom, and in a way, we did. It certainly felt like it.

We'd ride our bikes down hot paved roads to friends' houses, knocking on screen doors in our cut-off shorts and faded tank tops, hair tangled from the wind, before racing off again, barefoot and wild, toward the lake. We'd toss our bikes onto the sand without a second thought and leap off the docks into the cool, glittering water. We shared everything—friends, summer crushes, secrets whispered under blankets, and inside jokes that left us breathless with laughter. It was simple, beautiful, and untouched by the weight of growing up. Pure in a way I didn't recognize until much later.

We were dressed the same until we could find the words to say otherwise, the same clothes, just different colors. Her favorite was blue. Mine was purple, sometimes pink. I'm not sure I even had a favorite color. I think I just picked one so I wouldn't seem weird next to her strong certainty. We used to joke at Christmas, "Same thing, different color!" and we'd mean it with love. We were alike, but not identical— brown eyes to her blue, brunette to her blonde.

Once when we were just three- and four-years-old, we went to a Halloween party as a farmer and his wife. Robyn wore a bonnet and lipstick. I wore a fake mustache and plaid shirt, my hair had just been cut into a pixie after I decided to chop it myself. I won first prize in the boys' costume category. "Great costume, son," the man said as he handed me a plastic pony. "I'm a girl," I said. It might've been the first time I spoke my truth and got patted on the head and dismissed. But I remember Robyn beside me, proud and smiling.

As we got older, something subtle started to change between us, not in love, but in direction. We were still the Gorrie girls, still sisters to the bone. But slowly, we started becoming our own people. The kind of growing apart that happens not from conflict, but from becoming.

Robyn was grounded. Steady. A homebody in the most comforting sense of the word. She found peace in routine, in the familiar rhythm of our small-town life. She wasn't searching for more, she was content in the here and now. She didn't fuss about how she looked, never cared much for makeup or fashion trends. She was comfortable in her skin long before I ever knew what that meant.

I, on the other hand, felt pulled by something bigger—by bright lights, by cities I'd only seen in magazines and on TV, by the curiosity of what else was out there. I was always drawn to the edges of things, to possibility. I loved dressing up, doing my hair, experimenting with makeup, daydreaming about a life beyond the one we knew. I craved movement. Change. A story that hadn't been written yet.

We played on the same high school basketball team for a while. Tall, lanky, awkwardly graceful girls running the court. Robyn was the better player by far. She was strong, quick, focused, you could count on her when it mattered. I held my own, but let's be honest, I was more concerned with how I looked in my uniform than how many points I scored. People used to tease, "Your shot didn't go in, but it looked good!" Robyn's shot went in. That was just the kind of person she was, determined capability. No need for show.

And yet, despite those differences, we never drifted in love for each other. We may have started building separate lives, forming our own friendships, chasing different dreams, but the thread between us never snapped. When one of us was alone, the other was always the place to land. That's the thing about growing apart in proximity, you might not walk the same path, but you still carry the same map.

She was my sister. My anchor. My mirror, and my opposite.

And even as we became different versions of ourselves, she, rooted and steady, me, restless and reaching, we never stopped being us.

Of course, we fought. Over clothes. Over the phone. Physically, sometimes. And being the older one by twelve months, I always got in trouble. "You should know better," they'd say.

I'll never forget the day our dad finally gave us our own phone line. It felt like winning the lottery.

For years, we had monopolized the house phone, dragging the world's longest cord from room to room, winding it around doorways and down the hall as we chatted for hours with our friends. It was a constant negotiation, "Hurry up, I need the phone!" and a frequent source of frustration for our parents, especially our dad, who could never get through when he called home. We'd be deeply immersed in conversations about absolutely nothing, school gossip, boys, favorite songs, and yet it all felt so important.

When the technician came to install our very own line upstairs, we hovered like excited puppies. That phone wasn't just a phone, it was status. It was proof that we were growing up. Our bedroom took up the entire top floor of the house, a shared sanctuary filled with side-by-side waterbeds, matching desks, a little TV, and now… a phone. With our own number. Our own ring.

And then came the prank phone calls. Once we had our own phone, free from hovering parents, we felt a new kind of freedom. No one monitoring our calls. No one telling us to wrap it up. Just us, a dial tone, and a wild sense of possibility.

"Is your refrigerator running?" we'd ask the poor soul whom we randomly dialed, in our most serious voices. "Yes?" the person would say, confused. "Well, you better go catch it!" And then we'd slam the phone down and burst into uncontrollable giggles, rolling on the floor in the kind of laughter that only makes sense when you're twelve and your whole world is still wrapped in innocence. It was silly, harmless mischief to us.

Between having the top floor to ourselves, and now our own phone, it felt like we had our own apartment.

We answered every call like it might change our lives. And if we were downstairs and the phone rang? We sprinted, full tilt up the stairs, sometimes racing each other, breathless and tripping over ourselves just to be the one to say "Hello?"

We'd stay up late, lying on our beds with the lights off, cords stretched across the room, whispering into the receiver about crushes and weekend plans, interrupting each other with bursts of laughter. Those were the kinds of nights that stitched us together.

There was a window in our bedroom that led out to the roof over the sunroom below and we discovered we could pull the phone cord just far enough to climb out there with it. So we did. We'd sit under the stars with the receiver pressed to our ears, giggling with friends and feeling like queens of the world. It was wild, rebellious, and so completely us.

Until one afternoon, mid-conversation, I felt the phone cord tug tight. Slowly, it started pulling me back through the window. I turned around and realized my dad was winding the cord from the base. "How did you even know I was out there?" I asked, completely busted. "Because I drove by and saw you," he said, shaking his head.

Even now, I can still feel that feeling of the wind on our faces, the sound of our laughter, the giddy thrill of being young and full of possibility. That kind of wild abandon that stays with you.

We spent summers fishing and boating with our parents, especially during my dad's two weeks off. It became our rhythm, camping on islands, cooking over fires, water skiing across glassy lakes, disappearing into the water until our skin was wrinkled and our cheeks and noses freckled in the sun. Robyn and I would sit on the boat's edge, feet dangling in the water, pointing out clouds and telling stories, just the two of us and the sound of summer. Those days felt endless in the best way.

Tucked deep in the woods was a place we couldn't wait to return to each summer—our day camp. Every August, it became our world for two unforgettable weeks. We would spend two magical weeks at a place that felt like its own little world. The bus would pick us up and drop us off at the top of a long trail, and we'd hike ten to fifteen minutes through thick woods to reach the camp. To this day, if I catch the scent of damp moss or morning dew on a forest trail, I'm transported back to that hike, backpacks bouncing, the sun peeking through the trees, that earthy mix of pine needles and damp soil greeting us like an old friend.

The camp was tucked along the edge of the water, and it was full of activities, archery, crafts, judo, gymnastics, and every summer, a musical performance where we'd lip-sync and dance our little hearts out. I played Sandy from Grease one year and thought I was the coolest girl in the world.

Robyn and I were always in the same group. We had the same friends, liked the same things, and looked out for each other without needing to say it. That was just our way.

Every year, there was one overnight campout where we slept in rustic wooden cabins with bunk beds. It was a big deal and Robyn and I always claimed two top bunks, side by side, joining our friends in a line of whispered secrets and late-night laughter. We'd stay up late, telling ghost stories and daring each other to peek out the windows into the dark.

But one night, as the stories died down and the moonlight crept across the cabin floor, I tried to climb down to go to the bathroom. My foot slipped. I lost my balance and fell hard, flat on my face. I remember the thud, the shock, the silence before the counselors rushed over, and Robyn's voice crying, panicked echoing through the cabin. "Is she okay?!" I had a fat lip and a bruised ego, but I was fine. Robyn wasn't. Not until she knew for sure. Because if I was hurt, she was hurt. She wouldn't leave my side.

We both loved swimming, but that was one place we differed. I was a strong swimmer, the kind who zipped through badge levels and couldn't wait to dive into the deep end. Robyn... not so much. She was a good swimmer, safe and steady, but she just couldn't pass her blue badge. Year after year, she stayed stuck there, and it became this light-hearted family joke, the girl who could do flips off the dock but just couldn't master that blue badge.

Robyn, of course, teased me relentlessly about my crush on Ray and how I followed him around like a lost puppy. We would dissolve into laughter about it, but I knew she secretly admired my ability to be a good enough swimmer to be a co-coach with Ray. And in those moments, even as we were growing into our own people, even as we started to have our own stories, our own crushes, our own little separations, we were still side by side. Both proud of each other, worried for each other, and still intricately connected.

We were becoming our own people, yes, but we were never apart.

When we were old enough to start working summer jobs, it became clear just how different Robyn and I really were becoming, yet somehow, it brought us closer. I landed a job waitressing at the truck stop just off the highway and fell in love with it instantly. I thrived in the buzz of it all, the clatter of dishes, the flow of coffee, the constant stream of people passing through on their way to somewhere far more exciting than our little town.

I remember one day, a professional football team pulled in for lunch on their way to an away game. For a small-town girl like me, it felt like something out of a movie. They were so full of energy, confidence, and charisma. They teased me gently, getting a kick out of my innocence, and started teaching me their slang, rhythms and expressions I'd never heard before.

Robyn, true to who she was, worked at the gas bar pumping fuel. Our jobs were a perfect reflection of our personalities. I dove headfirst into the social buzz, and she found calm in routine, quiet conversations, and independence. But no matter where our differences showed up, we always came back to each other.

I still remember the first time I drove after getting my license. Of course, I took Robyn with me. We were heading to my boyfriend's house the next town over, a simple country drive that felt like a rite of passage. Somewhere along the stretch of road, a rabbit darted out in front of us, and I had no time to react. I hit it. We both screamed and instinctively closed our eyes. I snapped mine open a second later, still behind the wheel, heart pounding. We were devastated.

Robyn turned to me and said, "Oh my god, you killed that rabbit."

"I know," I yelled back, my stomach in knots.

She tried to comfort me, reminding me of what Dad always said, that you can't swerve, you have to just keep going. I knew that was true. But it didn't make it feel any better. The whole moment is burned into my memory for how we held each other in the panic and heartbreak.

When I moved out at seventeen, I didn't fully understand what it would mean for Robyn. For the first time in her life, I was gone. Just like that, no warning, no slow goodbye. One day I was there, and the next I wasn't.

She had only known life with me in it, sharing bedrooms, campfires, secrets, and everyday sisterhood. And then suddenly, she had to learn how to live without me. I can only imagine how hard that must have been for her, and I've carried the guilt of that departure ever since. I didn't mean to leave her alone. I just didn't know back then what it would cost her or what it would mean to me, years later, when I finally understood the depth of what we had.

Even with all the distance that eventually stretched between us, me chasing something bigger in Los Angeles, Robyn still living at home in our small town, our connection never loosened. It would always find a way to thread itself back into the ordinary moments.

One night, I got a call from her. It wasn't late, but I could hear something in her voice the second I picked up.

"Can your face fall asleep before you do?" she asked. Her tone was half-joking, but underneath it, I heard the real question, the fear she was trying to keep tucked inside.

She didn't have to explain. I knew exactly what she meant. We had grown up watching for symptoms in ourselves most kids didn't even know existed. Ever since our mom was diagnosed with multiple sclerosis when we were young, our lives had been marked by a vigilance. We were the kind of children who noticed limps, tremors, numbness. We knew the signs. We'd learned to pay attention.

So when Robyn called to ask me about her face, what she really wanted to know was: Could this be it? Could this be happening to me too?

I tried to reassure her, to be the calm voice she needed in that moment, even as my own stomach twisted. I told her it could be anything, sleeping funny, a pinched nerve, stress as she was writing exams. But behind my words was the same unspoken fear I knew lived in both of us, the fear that maybe we wouldn't outrun it. That maybe we were next.

Looking back, I realize how much we carried from such a young age. That call was about more than a tingling face. It was about being sisters in a world that had taught us how fragile the body could be, and how closely we needed to watch it. It was about needing each other to say, "You're okay," even when we weren't sure.

All that watchfulness came at a cost. We learned to scan and to worry, but not to rest. I didn't know how to soothe myself, only how to brace for the next thing that might go wrong.

That night, I comforted Robyn the best I could. Years later, I realized I needed to learn how to offer that same kind of comfort to myself.

It would be a few years before the doctors officially confirmed it, but deep down, that phone call was the beginning. When the diagnosis came, multiple sclerosis, it wasn't a surprise, but that didn't make it any easier.

Robyn had always suspected it. I used to tell her she was paranoid, that she didn't have it, that she was overthinking every tingle or ache. I wanted to believe that. I needed to believe that. Because the alternative was too cruel to imagine.

And yet, when it was confirmed, it was Robyn who held herself with calm, not the kind that comes from peace, but the kind that comes from preparing. From knowing this day would eventually come. She'd been watching it happen to our mother for most of her life. She knew what MS could take.

But we were ten years further along from our mother's diagnosis. I clung to that. I told her things were different now. There were new treatments, better research, more hope. I believed that. I believed there was still a life ahead of her, not just an existence, but a life. And Robyn believed it, too. She had to.

She became a fighter.

She was determined to slow the disease, to prove it wouldn't define her. She tried everything. Food protocols, exercise, medications, mindfulness, stem cell therapy in other countries. She researched endlessly, read everything she could, and followed every possible path with unwavering commitment. She refused to go down without trying everything.

But MS is a thief. It takes slowly, in pieces. First, it steals your ease. Then your strength. Then your independence. And through it all, she held her dignity. Her humor. Her stubbornness. But I could see the burden in her eyes, the frustration of a body that was no longer hers to trust.

There's a helplessness that comes with watching someone you love suffer. I couldn't fix it. I couldn't slow it down. I couldn't take it from her. And so I just tried to love her through it, even when our lives were running in opposite directions.

I had two boys. A job that demanded everything from me. A marriage. A life that didn't allow for weekly visits or long afternoons together. We lived a few hours apart, and sometimes that felt like an ocean. But we stayed connected the way we always had, through late-night calls and heart-to-hearts that skipped over small talk and went straight to what mattered.

Still, the guilt crept in.

I wasn't there enough. Not like I wanted to be. Not like I should have been.

But Robyn never held that against me. If anything, she held space for me, for my busy life, for my complicated world, for the way we were still tethered, even when time and distance pulled us apart.

She never asked for more than I could give. But God, I wish I had given more anyway.

After her diagnosis, Robyn kept moving forward. Strong, steady, determined to live.

She finished her post-secondary education and graduated with a degree in psychology. She got a job as a parole officer, work that required both grit and compassion, two things she had in abundance. And then, she and her partner began to build their dream home, a house nestled in the woods, surrounded by trees and space. It was exactly what Robyn always wanted. A place that felt like peace.

And then came the news, she was pregnant.

I had just had my oldest son Owen, so the timing couldn't have been more perfect. Our babies would be close in age, and the idea of raising cousins who would grow up like siblings made me so happy. She was due in August, right around our birthday. Robyn and I, born exactly one year apart on August 15th, could there be a more perfect full-circle moment?

I remember the phone ringing, and I picked it up immediately. "Happy birthday!" Robyn said, her voice light.

"Ugh," I groaned, teasing. "I thought you were calling to say your water broke!"

She paused. "Oh… and my water broke!"

We both screamed. "What?! What are you doing talking to me?! Go to the hospital!"

She laughed and told me her contractions were still far apart. We had already made a deal that I would be there, I would drive the three hours to support her through the birth. So I left Owen with my husband, jumped in the car, and hit the road with a full heart and butterflies in my stomach.

When I got to the hospital, I walked up to the nurse's station and explained who I was. The nurse smiled, then stepped away to speak with Robyn. A few moments later, she came back out.

"She doesn't want you to come in," she said gently.

"What?" I blinked. "Are you sure?"

I was confused, hurt, maybe even a little angry. I'd driven all this way. I had promised I'd be there. My sister needed me. But I sat down anyway, unsure of what else to do, disappointment settling heavily in my chest.

Moments later, I heard the squeak of wheels. They were moving her toward the delivery room, and as she passed me in the hallway, our eyes locked.

And that's when I saw it.

Terror.

Complete, wide-eyed, breath-stealing fear.

The nurse turned around and quickly backtracked. "Actually, she wants you!"

I ran in without hesitation, straight to her side. I grabbed her hand and looked into her eyes. "I've got you, sis," I whispered.

She stared right back at me, her voice trembling. "I've changed my mind. I can't have this baby."

And then we both laughed and cried. She told me the epidural window had closed, and the nurses wouldn't give her anything. "I can't do this," she repeated over and over. "Erin, I can't. I can't," she kept saying over and over as she tried to get up off the bed looking like she wanted to run as fast as she could out of this moment.

But I knew this version of Robyn. I'd seen her before, on skating rinks and basketball courts and camping trips. The girl who always finished what she started. She just needed someone to anchor her. And that was my job.

"Yes, you can," I told her. "You will. And if you do it in the next couple hours, your baby will share our birthday. Can you imagine that?

Another Gorrie, born on the same day."

A few pushes later, she was born.

A perfect six-pound, two-ounce baby girl.

Born on August 15th.

Our day. It was nothing short of a miracle.

The moment Robyn laid eyes on her daughter, the fear was gone. In its place was a love so full, so consuming, I could feel it in the walls.

Watching my sister, after everything, after MS, after heartbreak, after doubt, hold her daughter for the first time, is a moment etched into the deepest corners of my heart. It is one of the greatest gifts of my life.

From terror to triumph, from pain to pure love, I was there for all of it. And I'll carry it with me forever.

When she told me she was choosing Medical Assistance in Dying, I lost it.

"No," I cried out. "You can't do this to me. You can't do this to your daughter."

I was shaking. My throat burned. The room started to spin, everything in me was fighting to reject what I'd just heard. But Robyn... she was calm. So heartbreakingly calm. Her voice over the phone, a deep unwavering peace that made it all the more unbearable.

"Erin," she said softly, "I'm not living. I'm existing."

Those words, simple, quiet, and devastating shattered me.

Unbeknownst to me she had already been through a year of consultations, therapy, paperwork, and soul-searching. She'd thought it through more thoroughly than anyone could imagine. And then she told me the date she had chosen, October 22nd. The same day our mom died.

"That way," she said, gently, "you only have to mourn on one day."

I screamed. I sobbed. I begged her. I told her I'd move in, take care of her, give up everything. I'd drop my life and wrap mine around hers, just to keep her here.

"This isn't living," she repeated.

Those final six weeks… they were the most agonizing, sacred, love-filled moments we had shared in years.

We sat side-by-side and combed through her affairs, like two little girls whispering secrets under a blanket fort but this time, the secrets were final wishes. She wrote letters, chose gifts, and planned every detail with a grace I can only hope to carry one day.

We cried until our bodies hurt.

We laughed until we forgot why we were crying.

And one day, she looked at me with this glowing softness and said, "This is all I ever wanted, to spend time with you." God, I hold that close. I hold it like a fragile shell in my hands, careful not to let the sharp edge of guilt crack it. Because she wouldn't want that. She would hate that.

She didn't want a funeral. "I want a living celebration of life," she told me. "While I'm still here to enjoy it."

So we gave her one. One week before the date.

A backyard barbecue, with music and sunshine and everyone she loved. There were tears, yes, but there was laughter too. There were hugs that lingered, shared memories, goofy photos, and a kind of bittersweet joy that only comes when you know time is running out.

And then…

The day came.

One by one, we were invited into her room to say our goodbyes. I had been sitting on the floor beside her bed, knees drawn up, arms around my legs, trying to hold in the pain. Beside me was my niece—Robyn's daughter, now seventeen years old. On the other side sat Robyn's best friend, and nearby was Robyn's partner. I stayed close, bearing witness as people quietly entered and exited, their faces etched with sorrow, their hearts wide open. Some whispered. Some wept. Some sat in silence, brushing her hair or holding her hand like it might anchor her here a little longer.

She had asked for her partner and daughter to be with her at the very end. I couldn't have done it. I couldn't be there when the final breath left her body. But I also couldn't be far. My body felt too heavy to move, too wired to rest.

And then, my dad walked in. He moved toward her slowly, deliberately. As he leaned over her, Robyn tilted her head toward him and smiled, still her, still playful, even now.

"I was your favorite, right?" she asked with a glimmer in her eye. We both held our breath. Waiting. Needing to hear it.

"Yes," he said. Thank God he said yes.

Then it was my turn.

I knelt beside her, every part of me screaming against what I knew I had to do. I leaned in, eyes brimming with tears, and whispered, "If you've changed your mind… it's okay. No one will be mad."

She looked at me with this deep, quiet peace. "I'm not scared," she said.

And that was it. That was when the pain became something more, it stopped sitting quietly and started reshaping me.

I sobbed as I kissed her face over and over, trying to memorize every inch of her. I pressed my forehead to hers, breathing her in, my arms wrapped around her like I could somehow hold her soul in her body if I just squeezed tightly enough. I didn't know how to let go. How to physically tear myself away knowing I would never feel her warmth again, never hear her voice, never see her eyes light up at something ridiculous I said.

She kissed me softly and whispered, "Look for dimes. That'll be me."

And then I stood.

Somehow.

I walked out of that room on legs that didn't feel like mine.

And I collapsed.

I howled. This raw, guttural sound that exploded from deep inside me. A sound I didn't know I could make. A sound I didn't know anyone could make. It was primal. Grief in its purest form.

She passed with grace. With dignity. On her own terms. In a world that gave her no choices, she carved one out for herself.

And now, I see dimes in the strangest places.

I still talk to her. I feel her when the house is quiet, when the sun comes through the window just right, when I need her and I swear I hear her laugh tucked into the stillness.

Her daughter is so much like her in spirit which keeps her close. Sometimes when she laughs, it cuts me open and heals me all at once.

We will always be the Gorrie girls.

There will always be a part of my heart that belongs to Robyn.

And a part that is missing.

But I know she is free.

I know she's with our mom.

And I know, with everything I am, that she is still with me.

Always.

THE
BEST
PARTS
OF
ME

Before my boys, I was drifting. A ship without a rudder, moving but never arriving anywhere. Days blurred together in a numb rhythm.

I longed for something to tether me, something to make me feel like my life mattered. I wanted connection, meaning, a reason to get up that felt like more than obligation. But I didn't have a model for what that looked like. My mom, sick for most of my adolescence, couldn't be that anchor. My grandma did her best, but I still felt unmoored. I tried to fill the ache with busyness, with achievement, with being the dependable one everyone could count on. It worked, sometimes, for a little while. But none of it stayed. None of it filled me.

And though I couldn't name it then, what I was really starving for was love. Not the romantic kind, not even friendship. The kind of unrestricted, unconditional love that makes you feel like you belong somewhere. The kind of love that makes you feel safe to stop pretending.

Then Owen arrived, and everything shifted.

The delivery room was too bright, with a fluorescent glare that made everything feel sharper than it already was. My body shook from exhaustion, sweat clinging to my skin, my heart pounding from the hours of labor. I remember the cacophony of sounds, the multiple beeping monitors, the shuffle of nurses, my own shouts of pain, the low murmur of instructions I was half-hearing, half-drifting past. And then, suddenly, silence.

And into that silence, a cry.

They placed him on my chest, this tiny, squirming, red-faced bundle. His fists clenched as if he already knew he was going to fight his way through the world. His skin was warm and slick against mine, his breath uneven, and when his eyes fluttered open for just a second, it felt like he was looking straight through me. Anchoring me. Claiming me.

Time split cleanly in two. There was "the before" the drifting, untethered, going-through-the-motions me. And there was "the after", the me who suddenly had a purpose, a tether, a reason that pulsed through every part of me.

Holding him, I felt like I mattered. That my life suddenly had meaning. That I was here for a reason. His tiny body against mine was proof of it. The missing piece I'd been unknowingly searching for was right there in my arms.

And it was terrifying. Love this fierce felt dangerous, like it could undo me. What if I failed him? What if I wasn't enough? What if I couldn't do this? But no matter what the answers were to those questions, I knew I would give everything I had to keep him safe.

When Owen was born, he saved me in ways he'll never fully understand. He gave me a direction, a center of gravity, a reason to get up and keep moving. I wasn't drifting anymore. I belonged somewhere. With him. Regardless of where "where" was, with him I knew I belonged. Our love and connection remade me.

Leaving the hospital felt surreal. I had arrived as one person and was now leaving as someone else entirely. The hallways were full of activity but I felt like the world around me was moving in slow motion. My body was sore, every step reminding me of what I had just gone through, but I barely noticed. I was too aware of the tiny bundle strapped into the car seat I was carrying. That was now my world.

I remember standing outside the hospital doors, the automatic glass sliding closed behind me, and walking into an unknown world. I recognized everything, of course, but how I saw it was now different. The world looked sharper. Brighter. Even the trees seemed to stand taller.

The drive home was the longest of our lives. Every bump in the road felt like a threat. Every car that passed too closely made me tense up. I kept twisting around in the passenger seat to check that his chest was still rising and falling, that his tiny fists hadn't slipped out of the blanket. The responsibility was enormous, growing more substantial with each turn of the wheel

My world was so inextricably altered by Owen's existence that nothing at all was the same. Even walking into our home that we'd left just days before, with the very same walls, furnishings, and decor, was something else now. I walked through the house and laid him in the bassinet we had set up in the corner of our room, and then just stood there, staring. The silence was broken by the smallest of sounds, a sigh, a rustle, a tiny vocal squirm. Those sounds were everything.

That night, I didn't sleep. Not really. I couldn't settle. I sat up in bed, the soft light of the lamp casting shadows across the room, watching his chest rise and fall. Every few minutes I'd lean over to listen, to make sure. Exhaustion clung to me, but so did awe.

By the time I was pregnant with Oscar, I thought I had figured out love. Owen had already stretched me in ways I didn't know were possible, filling corners of my heart I hadn't even known were empty.

I'd lie awake at night, one hand resting on the curve of my stomach, listening to the soft rhythm of Owen's breathing in the next room, and wonder: How could I ever love another child as much as I loved him? It seemed impossible. My heart was already overflowing. The thought of dividing that love felt like a betrayal, like someone was going to lose.

And then Oscar arrived.

The room was dimmer this time, quieter. I was more aware—of my body, of the people around me, of the familiar ache and urgency of bringing life into the world. When they laid him in my arms, time slowed again, but in a different way. I expected to feel torn between two loves, but instead, my heart did something I didn't know it could do. It stretched. Wider. Bigger. Deeper.

His cry was softer than Owen's had been, a little whimpering wail that calmed the instant I whispered his name. His fingers curled around mine, impossibly small, impossibly sure. Right there, I understood, love doesn't divide. It multiplies.

Looking into his eyes, I felt my heart expand, making room for him without taking anything from his brother. It was like discovering an entirely new wing of the house you thought you knew by heart. More space. More light. More love.

I realized I hadn't reached the edge of love at all. There was no edge. No limit. Love could grow and stretch endlessly. And with Oscar, it did.

My boys gave me the love I had ached for all my life. In their laughter, in their arms wrapped tight around my neck, in the simple way they called me Mom, I felt something unconditional I had never known.

And because I knew the ache of not being mothered myself, I mothered them the way I always longed for.

I didn't have a blueprint to follow. My mom had been sick for most of my childhood, and though she loved me in her own way, her illness kept her preoccupied. I grew up without that everyday sense of being someone's priority.

So when I became a mother, I built for my boys what I had missed.

I became their solid ground. I wrapped them in love. I created rituals, traditions, safe places. Not because I knew how, but because I knew what not having it felt like.

Bedtime stories, even when I was exhausted, so their last memory of the day was my voice beside them. I can still see Oscar, clutching his blanket, whispering "one more" when I'd already read three. His eyes would flicker, heavy with sleep, but he just wanted me there a little longer. And even though my body begged for rest, I'd turn the page and keep reading, because I knew what it felt like to want someone to stay and not have them.

Sunday pancake breakfasts, messy and loud, where it wasn't really about the food but about the table we all gathered around. Movie nights with popcorn on the couch, the lights turned low so the room itself felt safe.

The best nights were the dance parties. Music blaring, the boys spinning until they collapsed in giggles, me flailing right along with them. Bills, work, exhaustion, they all disappeared. All that was left was us, barefoot on the living room floor, turning an ordinary night into magic.

I didn't even notice it happening, but slowly and deliberately, I wove my whole world around being their mom. It was in the way I planned my days around their needs, the way their laughter became my oxygen. Every thread of my life pulled toward them until I could no longer tell where they ended and I began.

When Owen left for university, the ache was immediate. Pride and grief tangled together as I hugged him goodbye and watched him walk away, backpack slung over his shoulder, already half in his new life. I held it together until I got back in the car, but as soon as I shut the car door, the tears came hot and heavy. The road blurred as I drove, my chest heavy with grief I wasn't fully expecting. He wasn't gone forever, but the house felt different the second I stepped back inside. One less plate at the dinner table. One less towel hanging in the bathroom. The silences were more common with one less person in the house.

But Oscar was still home, and I clung to that. The house still had rhythm, still had noise, still had purpose. I still had someone to wait up for, someone leaving hats and socks in corners, someone whose presence reminded me that motherhood was still my daily role.

And then Oscar left.

That's when the bottom dropped out. The silence was suffocating, not just quiet but hollow. I remember standing in the laundry room staring at the basket, empty for the first time in decades. No socks, no jeans, no shirts carrying the faint scent of cologne or sweat. Just nothing. I'd catch myself listening for his music, only to be met with nothing. Just quiet. I couldn't breathe.

David was there, of course. We were both navigating this new space, both figuring out how to live in a house that suddenly felt too big for just the two of us. He tried to soften it for me, suggesting dinners out, planning little getaways, but the truth was, it wasn't about the empty house. It was about me.

For more than twenty years, my identity had been woven into theirs. My purpose, my meaning, my very sense of self was anchored in being their mom. Without the daily chaos, the lunches to pack, the games to cheer at, the late-night talks, I didn't know who I was.

The grief wasn't just about missing them. It was about missing myself.

At first, I tried to outrun it—cleaning, scrolling, keeping myself busy. But eventually the quietude pressed in enough that I had to stop and listen. And in that listening, I realized, I had no idea who Erin was outside of being Mom.

It was disorienting, terrifying, and somewhat freeing. And these feelings encompassed my relationship with David. Our marriage had been built in the rhythm of raising kids together, two parents orbiting around the center of our boys. When that center shifted, we had to figure out who we were to each other without the constant activity of parenting in the background. And I had to figure out who I was, period.

The silence that once felt unbearable slowly began to shift into space. And in that space, I started to find myself. I gave myself permission to rest, to breathe, to unroll my yoga mat again. I picked up my pen and started writing. I learned what I liked again, not as Mom, not as wife, but as Erin.

Motherhood gave me purpose. It gave me the unconditional love I'd always yearned for. It gave me a home, belonging, purpose. But in their leaving, my boys gave me one more gift, the chance to meet myself.

THE
THIRD

I didn't think I could get pregnant.

Not because I couldn't biologically, I'd already had two beautiful boys. But because I knew my body. I had gone off the pill on purpose. I didn't want the hormones in me anymore. I trusted my cycle. I was regular like clockwork, and I believed I could predict the "safe" windows. I thought I had it under control. But somehow... I screwed it up.

I was at my friend's house when I told her I was late. She looked at me, concern soft in her voice, and asked, "Do you think you're pregnant?" I shook my head. I really didn't think I was. But something in me said: Take the test.

We drove to the pharmacy together. Two women in our thirties, mothers, wise in ways we hadn't been ten years before, but here we were, buying pregnancy tests like teenagers. I trusted her with my life. She had been with me through so much, my separation, raising the boys, rebuilding after heartbreak. We met when my sons were still little and she was pregnant with her twins. Our friendship had roots.

I bought more than one test. One wasn't going to be enough.

Back at her house, I walked into the bathroom and peed on the stick. I placed it on the counter and came out to set the timer. Those few minutes felt like an eternity. We sat in silence, not knowing what to say. When the time was up, I walked back in and saw two lines.

Pregnant.

No. That couldn't be right.

I took two more. All positive.

I felt numb. Disoriented. How could this be happening? I was in my mid-thirties. I had two children. I was finally working toward my dream of becoming a police officer. I was pouring myself into the application process with everything I had.

Pregnancy didn't fit into that picture. Not even close.

I didn't give David a choice. I told him I was pregnant, and in the same breath, I said I wasn't keeping the baby. I didn't want to have a conversation. I had already decided.

It wasn't out of cruelty. It was out of urgency.

I was clawing my way toward something I believed would save us all. A career that would provide stability, income, identity. I had two boys depending on me. I didn't see how I could possibly bring another baby into the world and still hold everything together.

I searched for clinics. Shame washed over me in waves. How am I in my mid-thirties and I'm having an abortion? I felt foolish. Embarrassed. Like I should've known better. I told myself no one could ever know. Just my friend. Just David. That was it.

I found a clinic in the city and booked the appointment. David offered to come with me. At first, I told him I'd go alone. I had convinced myself I was tough, that I could handle anything. But when he said he'd come, I was grateful. I just didn't let myself say that out loud.

We drove to the appointment. I remember feeling small, dirty, ashamed. Protesters stood outside the clinic, their signs and glares pressed down on me adding to a burden that already felt unbearable. Once inside, I filled out the forms, paid the fee, and waited.

David wasn't allowed into the procedure room, so a nurse sat next to me and held my hand. She was gentle and warm. I held on to her like a lifeline.

The doctor explained what would happen, a vacuum procedure. I shut my eyes as tight as I could and tried not to think. I told myself to be strong. I was going to be a police officer, for God's sake. I could get through this.

But as the machine started and I felt the tugging and pressure, a wave of grief threatened to swallow me. It reminded me of giving birth to Owen, when they had to turn him while I was pushing. It brought back the helplessness, the pain, the vulnerability.

Only this time, I wouldn't be leaving with a baby in my arms.

When it was over, I felt hollow. I got dressed, walked out, and told myself it was done. Over. I had done what I needed to do.

But a part of me stayed behind in that room. The part that didn't have time to cry. The part that couldn't process what had just happened because there was too much to hold. I left the clinic physically lighter, but emotionally, something had anchored itself deep inside me.

David drove me home. He had to leave shortly after, and I remember sitting alone in my house, sore and hollow, my body cramping with discomfort, every movement a reminder of what I'd just been through. The next day, we spoke on the phone. He heard it in my voice, that I was trying to be strong but barely holding on. Before I could ask, he showed up at my door. That meant more than I ever told him.

I moved forward quickly. I had to. The bleeding passed. I went back to pretending like nothing happened. A few weeks later, I flew out west to spend time with my Nana after my Grandpa passed.

On the flight home, I started cramping badly. I tried to breathe through it, to pretend it was nothing. But as the plane began its descent, I knew something wasn't right. As soon as we landed, I bolted to the nearest airport bathroom. I was bleeding uncontrollably. I stood there in a stall, frozen, the chaos of the terminal just outside the thin metal door. My hands trembled. My stomach turned. My thoughts raced. Thank God I was wearing dark pants. But nothing could hide what was happening inside of me.

I got myself to my girlfriend's house, and she went with me to the hospital. I had to say the words out loud, I had an abortion a month ago. I felt so exposed. So ashamed. But the doctor reassured me, it was normal. Nothing to worry about. His words should have settled me, but they didn't. Because what I carried wasn't just physical. It was the silence I'd wrapped around the whole thing. It was the grief that had nowhere to land.

I worried anyway. I grieved anyway. Quietly. Alone. I tucked it all inside, pretending I was fine, pretending it hadn't tore through something deep inside me. But at night, when the house was quiet, it hung over me like a shadow I couldn't shake. I didn't know how to name it, and I didn't know who to tell. So I carried it, silently, like so many other things in my life.

I stuffed down the pain. I told myself I had done the right thing, for my boys, for my future. I didn't let myself feel too much. I was afraid that if I really let it in, I'd never forgive myself.

To this day, when a doctor asks how many pregnancies I've had, saying "three" never gets easier. It catches in my throat. There's no space on the form to explain. No checkbox for the one I chose but still grieve. Just a number. Just clinical data. I say it anyway. I answer the question. But there's always a pause, an invisible moment where I hold my breath and wonder if they'll ask me to explain. And I pray they don't.

I don't regret my decision. It was what I had to do. But it doesn't mean it didn't change me.

With the overturning of Roe v. Wade, I've found myself thinking about that time in my life more often. What if I hadn't had the option? What if I was forced to carry a pregnancy I knew I couldn't handle? What if that choice had been taken from me?

It's terrifying.

And it's why I'm finally ready to speak this truth out loud:

Yes, I had an abortion.

Yes, I was already a mother.

And yes, I loved all three of my children, even the one I never got to hold.

There are things I've had to say to myself to heal, to move forward, to learn how to live with both the choice I made and the private grief that came with it. Words I return to when shame creeps in, when I find myself alone at night, lying awake in the quiet house, no distractions left to soften the ache.

That's when the old questions press the hardest. That's when I need to whisper back to myself:

You didn't mess up.
You were exhausted. You chose what you thought was right.
It broke your heart, and you grieved.
That didn't make you heartless. It made you human.
You weren't less of a mother. You were brave.

THE
GRIEF
I
WAS
TOO
AFRAID
TO
FEEL

There's a song I hear every now and then, often in a store or flicking through the stations on the radio. And when I do, I'm instantly transported back to a basement with cement floors and the faint musty smell of our unfinished home. I can see her, my mom, dancing through the moves of her women's fitness class, practicing with a fierce grace that only she had.

I'd sit on the floor, arms around my knees, watching in awe. Her leotard and leg warmers. Her crop top layered over it. Her joy. Her beauty. It all radiated out of her. She was vibrant. Alive. Fun.

My mom was so involved, so present in our lives when we were young. Wherever we lived, she showed up fully, for us, and for our community. She started play school co-ops, volunteered at the skating club, taught nursery school. She poured herself into making every place feel like home, not just for us but for everyone around her. And even with so much already on her plate, she went back to school to get her ECE diploma, determined to create a better life for us. Her energy, her presence, her exuberance for life, was everywhere in those early years.

Saturdays were always for cleaning. The smell of Windex and lemon Pledge can still transport me back instantly, as if I'm walking through our house again, watching sunlight catch the dust in the air while my mom moved from room to room. The sharp citrus scent clung to the air, seeping into every surface until it became the smell of comfort, of routine, of home. The vacuum hummed in the background, the steady back and forth rhythm of her work, while my sister and I were given our own little jobs—dusting end tables, tidying our rooms—in exchange for a few dollars of allowance. It didn't matter how small the task was, what mattered was that we were part of it, our little tasks blending into the chorus of her Saturday song. But as the years carried on, we noticed something was off.

It started with her wrist, then the other. She wore a pink splint and said she'd sprained it. But soon came the diagnosis, multiple sclerosis. To my sister and me, it may as well have been cancer. A disease meant something was wrong. Something dangerous. Something that killed you. And though we were told she wasn't dying, fear took root anyway.

Doctors' appointments. Whispers out of earshot. Subtle changes in her walk. Her thoughts. Her presence. Her balance. We weren't part of those conversations, likely to protect us, but when you're a child and no one tells you what's going on, you make up your own truth. And our truth was that we were going to lose our mom.

She needed a walker. Then a wheelchair. Still, she insisted on cooking dinner. She'd sit on her walker at the stove, peeling potatoes or stirring sauces. But there were burns. Falls. Accidents. Eventually, it wasn't safe for her to be alone. A helper came in the mornings, but she hated strangers in the house. She stopped answering the door. We all started having the hard conversations about long-term care.

When my dad found the first home, hours away, I drove there to see it. The moment I walked in, my stomach turned, it felt like an institution, cold and clinical. My mom was distraught. She deserved warmth, dignity, familiarity. Eventually, he found a closer place, one that felt gentler, but I still didn't feel part of the decisions. By then I was a couple of hours away, deep into my flying career, busy and gone often. My grandparents visited her nearly every week, and they became my source of updates. They loved her fiercely and didn't always agree with my dad's choices—especially because he had already moved on with someone else.

Before her illness, my mom and dad loved to go to dances. They would go out together and dance the night away, his eyes never leaving hers. He loved to dance with my mom. I can still picture the way they moved together, so in sync, so connected. To me, that was love. That was marriage.

So when my grandmother said it plainly, "Your dad needs to divorce your mom," it felt almost impossible to reconcile. Because my mom wasn't capable of legal decisions, the responsibility fell on me, her power of attorney. At barely thirty years old, I had to divorce my father on my mother's behalf. It was surreal. Traumatizing. I wanted to protect her from pain, to shield her from knowing about his new relationship. But I also felt like I was betraying her—severing a bond she would have never wanted broken. My dad had moved on, met someone at work, and begun building a new life with her. My grandparents wanted to protect my mom, believing she could live for many more years, and they were terrified about her future, her care, her assets. Divorcing my dad meant what was hers would remain hers.

What made it even more unbearable was knowing the truth of who my parents had been together. They adored each other. They were the loves of each other's lives. If she hadn't gotten sick, they never would have been divorcing. It was the disease that drove the wedge between them, not a lack of love. And I knew with every bone in my body that if my mom had known the marriage was legally over, that the man she had loved since she was young had moved on—it would have devastated her.

Her life already felt so tragic, so heartbreaking. She was barely in her fifties, living in a nursing home full of ninety year olds, her vibrancy stolen, her body betraying her. I told myself that keeping her from knowing was merciful. That I was protecting her, giving her dignity where life had already stripped so much away.

I felt guilty often knowing all of this while she didn't. I carried it in silence. The roles had turned, and now it was my job to shield her from pain. But the weight of it was crushing.

And it was made even harder by the fact that I had only just begun to rebuild a relationship with my dad. For so long, I had wanted his approval, wanted to feel close to him. And now, I was the one tasked with saying the words my grandparents believed my mom was entitled to—words that often upset him. Every conversation felt like I was being pulled in two directions. I didn't want to lose the fragile closeness I had finally found with my dad, but I couldn't abandon my responsibility to my mom either. It was an impossible position.

There were months of back-and-forth, endless difficult conversations that often ended with me in tears. I would hang up the phone and sob, feeling like no matter what I said or did, I was letting someone down. I was torn between my grandparents' urgency, my father's frustration, and my own aching heart.

In the end, the divorce went through. On paper, it was settled. But in my body, it never was. Even now, I can feel the density of it, the impossible burden of making choices that no daughter should ever have to make.

At the same time I started the process of having my mom move closer to me. I wanted her near. To visit her often. But the waitlist was years long. Then, one day, while teaching a fitness class, my phone rang. It was my sister. Her voice was barely recognizable, swallowed by sobs.

"Mom died."

The world dimmed. My legs went numb. The music in the studio faded into a muffled hum, like I was suddenly underwater. I couldn't breathe, couldn't think. My body felt suspended, as though time had stopped and left me floating outside myself.

And then the door opened. Women filed in, chatting, laughing, unrolling their mats. They looked to me for direction, for the steady voice of their instructor.

I didn't know what to do. My mother had just died, and I didn't even know how to stand, how to move, how to exist in that moment. Every part of me wanted to collapse. To scream. To run. But the part of me trained from childhood to please, to not be a problem, took over.

So I shoved the grief down, sealed it into a box inside my chest, and smiled. I walked to the front of the room, my voice calm, even as my insides screamed. I taught the class like nothing had happened, stretch after stretch, pose after pose, while my world had just shattered.

Because that's what I did back then. I didn't allow myself to break. I carried on for everyone else, even when it felt like I was collapsing inside.

Because I had to.

I had two small boys. I was separated. I was holding everything together with duct tape and grit. There was no room to break. No one else to carry things if I crumbled.

Once class was finished, I called my dad. He couldn't bring himself to go see her. He said he didn't want that to be his final memory of her.

So I went.

When I walked into the room, my uncle and grandfather were already there. My grandfather was seated beside her bed, gently stroking her hair the way you might soothe a child. My mother's face was pale. Eerily still. She didn't look like herself anymore—her vibrance, her warmth, all gone.

The nurses were crying. One of them touched my arm softly and said, "She passed suddenly, while we were bathing her. It was quiet. Peaceful. She didn't suffer."

I clung to those words, desperate to believe them. Peaceful. Calm. As good an ending as she could have had. But standing there, nothing about it felt peaceful to me. Her warmth, her presence, the love she always carried for me, it was gone. The room was cold, empty, and so was my heart.

I held it together until I got back to the car. And then I broke. I sobbed uncontrollably, the kind of guttural crying that makes you wonder if you'll ever stop, if you'll ever be able to breathe again. But eventually, I had to. The boys were waiting for me. I had to drive the two hours home and keep moving.

Her service brought no closure. Two weeks of waiting, planning, gathering family, and when it came, I still felt nothing but numbness. No peace. No finality.

And then, just weeks later, my grandmother died.

That loss hit like a second wave, crashing before I'd even caught my breath.

It was the cruelest blow. When my mom became too sick, my grandmother stepped in as a second mother to me, a steady, loving presence. She adored me, and I adored her back. And just the Christmas before, she had given me one of the most cherished memories of my life.

It was Christmas Eve. My boys were asleep. I was sitting in our little living room, enjoying an evening cocktail with my then husband and his parents, when we heard an unexpected knock on the front door. No one ever used that door, everyone knew to come to the back. I looked at him, confused, and went to answer it.

There stood my grandparents, grinning under reindeer antlers. "Surprise!" she said, twinkling. They stayed at a hotel nearby, just so they could be there Christmas morning to watch the boys open gifts. My house was full, alive, brimming with love. It was the best Christmas I ever had.

Losing my grandma just a month after my mom was like losing my mom all over again. Loss doubled over. And still, I didn't let myself grieve. I pushed it down. There was no space. No time. I locked it away and kept going. Because that's what I had always done. Because I didn't know how not to.

Then came Ray. And years later, Robyn. Each loss stacked on top of the other until the weight became unbearable. By the time my sister died, all the grief I had buried—my mom's, my grandma's, Ray's— erupted at once. I carried it all without letting myself feel it, without giving myself permission to break. I kept moving—through motherhood, through marriage, through policing, through every version of myself I thought I had to hold together.

When Robyn died, I finally broke. I was sitting in my car, parked in the driveway, hands locked around the steering wheel, gripping so tight it felt like my bones might snap. My chest heaved against a silence so thick it roared in my ears. The box I'd kept sealed inside me tore apart

The sobs came raw, ragged, unstoppable. It wasn't just Robyn, it was my mom, my grandma, Ray. It was the end of my marriage, the pieces of myself I had lost along the way. Years of grief I had shoved into a box burst out all at once, flooding the small space around me until I could hardly breathe.

Grief doesn't arrive in order. It waits. It stacks. It hides in the body until there's no more room to tuck it away. And when it erupts, it doesn't come at a convenient time. Mine came in the driveway that day, like an inheld breath finally released after years of holding it in.

It took me a long time to understand that grief isn't just about death. It's about the loss of dreams, of identities, of relationships, of the versions of ourselves we once knew and believed would last. And when we don't allow ourselves to feel it, our bodies carry it for us—quietly, relentlessly—until one day, we can't keep holding it anymore.

FINDING PUPPIES

T his is what healing feels like.

A warm puppy, tiny and breathy against your thighs, drifting in and out of sleep. A room full of people whose shoulders slowly uncurl. Laughter that starts as a ripple and becomes a tide. For an hour, the world outside the door doesn't matter; what matters is the small life in your lap and the way it makes your chest ease.

That's the experience that unfolds in my studio every time a class begins. People think it's about stretching or funny Instagram clips. It's so much more. It's about an invitation, gently, without pressure, to come back into your body. To remember how to feel. To find within yourself something that may have been missing for a while.

I know what people feel when they walk into my studio. I have felt the range of emotions they're likely experiencing. The uncertainty for what this all is, the hope that it will be joyful, the excitement to try something new yet somehow also familiar. I felt all of it the first time I walked into a studio for a puppy yoga class.

Oscar was in his first year of college, wrapped in the trepidation of stepping into a new life. He was moving through the world with the lingering hesitation of not ever really knowing the next right step and questioning every step he did take. He called one day and I heard the stress coming through in his voice. Oscar is my son who feels everything deeply so I wanted to see if there was something I could do to give him a little boost. I was looking for a low pressure class that we could do together. Something fun, familiar enough to be comforting, but also new enough to give him something to be excited to try. When puppy yoga popped up, I laughed, half in disbelief, half in hope. Puppies and yoga. Sounded like a winning combination.

We walked into the studio and I immediately felt myself relax. I turned to Oscar and he had a hint of a smile on his face, just one side tugging up slightly. The sun came through the windows a bit muted and watery. Bright enough to welcome you but not enough to make you squint. It felt sacred as I saw the light catch on the floating dust in the air. We unrolled our mats like we'd done a hundred times, but nothing about it felt ordinary. There were puppies, everywhere, tripping over one another, tails like tiny metronomes. Oscar's face softened in a way it hadn't in weeks. A smile that eventually appeared across his face was small and raw, hesitant and honest.

Then one of those wobbling puppies wandered over to me, climbed into my lap, circled once, and laid his head on my leg. His breath heavy against my hand and in a rush of emotion I hadn't expected, I started to cry.

Not ugly crying. Quiet, surprised, helpless tears that flowed soundlessly down my face. The tightness around my heart loosened like a knot finally detangling. I felt a soul-deep stillness come over me. All the while the tears kept coming. It felt like a pressure valve that had been opened. For a decade I had trained myself to detach, to tuck my emotions away to survive my job. That detachment was a tool, but it was also a loss. I hadn't known I'd grown so distant from myself until the puppy's sweet breath brought me back.

We left smiling, feeling lighter, more connected to the world around us. Oscar returned to school with more confidence. And I spent days thinking about the class and giggling to myself while I made my morning coffee. I didn't think I even knew how to giggle anymore. It was like finding a muscle I hadn't used in years and realizing, with a sudden exhilaration, I still had it.

Every time I thought of that puppy yoga class I would smile. The happiness and joy from the day would return. This in itself was remarkable considering the state of near-depression I had been existing in since I went off work three years prior. The class Oscar and I went to was two and a half hours away from me, so it wasn't a realistic option for me to go back regularly.

And then the craziest of thoughts started coming in. What if I offered puppy yoga classes here in my town? I'd been a fitness instructor off and on for years. I was a trained yoga instructor. I technically had all the qualifications to do it. But… could I? Would I? For months the answers were always an unequivocal no. No I would not be doing this.

But then the thoughts started hounding me. Why not? No really, why not? Why not here in town? Why not you?

Eventually the thoughts won over. I did the most ridiculous things. I found a studio. I found a breeder willing to help. I offered a class.

The first one was terrifying. I hadn't taught in years. My hands shook. Chaos was within me and all around me. The puppies arrived and the room dissolved into laughter and mayhem. As I stood in front of the class I saw people physically soften. Smiles lit up their faces. Shoulders dropped down from their ears. Knees fell a little bit more open. Giggles abound. Strangers reached across mats, offered tissues, traded stories, took photos for each other.

I watched all of this and thought back to my yoga class and I felt such pride and contentment. I'd offered to all these people the experience that had stayed with me for months and consumed most of my thoughts. I did this for them. I brought this joy to the people in my town. And this time when I noticed the muted, watery light, it was coming from within. I was filled with an inner glow. It felt like honesty. Of presence. Of alignment. As I stood at the front of the room, I realized I wasn't pretending to be anything other than exactly who I was.

I knew I had found something. I wasn't sure where it would lead but I knew that I wanted to keep doing it. I offered a few more classes. I got more comfortable teaching again. I started to create a routine around this being a more permanent part of my life. It felt wonderful to offer something that helped others while still helping myself. And the puppies… they brought such glee to each class, making the experience that much more wonderful.

One morning, I saw a few comments beneath a class video I had posted online that got under my skin. People were calling it a gimmick. Others wrote that it was "just cute" or worse, accused me of exploiting the puppies. The words bruised. But as I closed the computer and walked away for a while I started to wonder how someone could say something like that. How they could take something so meaningful and disparage it. Then I realized it was because they didn't see the deeper meaning. I wasn't sharing with them the deeper purpose behind the classes. Yes, each class I started with explaining how the class would go, what to expect with the puppies, and then led the class. But I wasn't sharing my story. Why it all mattered to me so much. Seeing those comments opened me up to seeing that it was time for me to go a step further. It was time to share with everyone why puppy yoga meant so much to me.

So when I stood before the class that week, I decided to share a bit more. I opened the class and said, "There are two things that happen in this room. One, the puppies come into a safe space to learn to socialize and build confidence. Two, there's a mental-health piece, being with animals helps people feel again." Then I took a deep breath and shared part of my personal story. I was a first responder. Five years ago I went off work after an incident that changed me. I created these classes for me because of how it felt healing to attend that first puppy yoga class and how I felt the same after one of my own classes. I explained how I felt connected to myself and to the larger world after spending an hour doing yoga and snuggling and playing with puppies, that I didn't feel so alone and isolated anymore. I told them that by offering these classes I was keeping the joy and connection alive. And mostly, I wanted them to have the opportunity to experience all of this too.

I expected awkward silence, maybe polite applause. What I got instead was people leaning forward, eyes wide and open, quietly telling me they understood. A nurse pulled me aside and told me, between sobs, that it was the first time she'd felt anything in months. A man told me he had stopped smiling until that morning. A mother said she felt whole in a way she hadn't since her child was born. It became clear to me that my willingness to be seen allowed others to down their own guard.

And the puppies, they do something human language cannot. They offer permission to be soft. They are relentless in their affection and stubborn in their innocence. They anchor people into the present with a power that therapists sometimes spend years trying to teach us to find. A hand on a puppy's back becomes a hand on your own heart. That bubbling laughter does more than lift your mood, it melts the tightness you've been holding and gives you a few moments of real ease.

I learned quickly that my studio was not just a room with mats and fur. It was a sacred place where people could reconnect with who they are inside and feel pure joy. For some, it was the first time they'd laughed without the cliff edge of dread on the horizon. For others, it was the first time they'd been seen and accepted without a title attached, not "Officer," not "survivor," not "caretaker," but simply themselves.

My classes have evolved over the two years. I now have my own studio rather than renting a space. I travel to different cities around the world and offer puppy yoga classes there. I offer our classes to groups who use them for healing. What was once a way to find peace, steadiness, and connection within myself has turned into a growing business. When I stop to take it all in, I shake my head in disbelief. I never could have imagined this for myself. And still, no matter how many classes I've taught, how many people I've met and puppies I've snuggled with, I still feel the same as I did at that very first class. This is how I know that our puppy yoga classes are more than "cute" or something made for Instagram. They are transformative.

I often think about a class that I ran at a first-responder treatment center. The center was beautiful, tucked deep into the pines and nestled in perfectly with the surrounding nature. It is a place where you can tell healing happens just by breathing the air. It's the kind of place that holds the weight of grief and hope in the same breath.

When I teach in treatment centers, it's tender and very personal. I see faces that carry the same hard edges I once wore, the same grief for what was lost and the tension of not knowing who you are because of it. I didn't have a steady, gentle place to go in those early days of trying to come back to myself, and that absence taught me how precious it is to be offered care. So when I stand there in front of fellow first responders with puppies and mats, I'm not just leading a class, I'm trying to be a single lighthouse for someone who might otherwise keep wandering. That feels like purpose.

Everyone who attended class that day had chosen to participate. As they walked in, the heaviness that they all carried was almost tangible. Collectively, there was personal torment weighing them all down. It felt like a fog had rolled in with them. But then the puppies arrived. Suddenly there was a break in the fog. It started to lift, ever so slightly.

There was a man, a veteran, I learned later, whose shoulders looked like they'd been welded in place. His jaw was clenched, his eyes distant. He moved through the postures like a machine set to function. One of the little puppies made a bee-line for him, unbothered by the armor the man wore. The puppy climbed into his lap and snuggled in like it had found home. At first the man ignored it, his movements exact and controlled. But the puppy would not leave.

Minute by minute, I watched his face change. He patted the puppy's head, and his shoulders eased, almost unnoticeable at first, then in a slow, visible exhale. At the end of class, he wrapped his arms around that beautiful ball of fur and for the first time all morning his eyes filled with something other than rage. He walked out with a different carriage, less burdened, no longer feeling like Atlas carrying the world. Later staff from the treatment center texted to say he hadn't stopped talking about it.

Every time I receive a message like that I am inclined to give all the credit to the puppies. They are magical, yes. But it's both the puppies and the space. It's the container of the class held with intention and care. It's the no-pressure invitation offered to allow yourself to feel. It's the puppies, it's the yoga, and it's so much more.

I didn't go into this thinking I was remaking my life. Honestly, in the beginning, I thought I was just creating something small that might make me smile more, bring joy back to my life. What it became was a mirror. The room reflected back the person I had been, the person who had been buried under duty and trauma and self-erasure. Creating these classes forced me to step into a life that fit not because someone else had prescribed it, but because it resonated in my bones.

I still have days when the old armor wants to slide back on. The past is loud and the symptoms show up without warning. Puppy yoga didn't erase any of that, and it wasn't a miracle cure, but a single, unexpected moment did open a door.

Over time the classes gave me something braver than relief, the nerve to say out loud who I am and why I started. I began with a puppy in my lap, and I kept going because each class handed me back that small, assured permission to be myself. Today I teach because people still arrive heavy and leave lighter, because the room keeps teaching me how to feel again, and because showing up for them is how I keep choosing myself.

RED HAIR

The light was soft in my new home office, quieted by the sheer curtains that dulled the glare of the afternoon. I leaned back in my chair, legs tucked under me, the air faint with fresh paint and lemon cleaner. My shoulders loosened for the first time all day. The room wasn't finished, not even close, but in that late-day glow, it felt like a promise—like maybe I was, somehow, claiming space in a life that finally felt like mine.

A couple of half-unpacked boxes sat near the door. Empty picture frames leaned against the wall, waiting to be filled. Shelves sat vacant as they silently watched to see what would adorn them. This room was for me It wasn't borrowed. It wasn't staged for someone else's comfort. It was mine.

I was creating a space that felt calm, soft, creative. The walls were painted a warm cream. The rug was plush under my bare feet. And there was a quiet energy in the air, not silence exactly, but a stillness that felt safe to settle into. Everything in that room had been chosen by me, for me. For the first time, I was in a space that reflected who I was becoming, not who I had to be.

I was going through a storage bin that I'd brought in and found something I hadn't thought about in years. It was so far removed from my life now that it was a memory that felt like it belonged in another lifetime. Tucked into the bottom of that storage bin was my old modeling portfolio.

I sat cross-legged on the floor and pulled it into my lap, the leather cover cool and familiar in my hands, worn from so many years of use. I had opened and closed that portfolio and carried it tucked at my side for years. I remembered immediately what was inside. I knew the order of the photographs. I knew the shoots that they were from. I knew the girl I was about to meet again. But I didn't expect the wave of tenderness for that girl on those pages that rose in my chest.

Page after page, there she was. Me, but not really.
Erin in her early twenties.
Eyes wide but guarded.
There was a facade of confidence in her posture, her stare, her angles.
Polished.
Practiced.
Professional.

But it wasn't true confidence; it was survival, dressed up as self-assurance. A performance I had been perfecting for most of my life.

The poses were mine, but the expressions were trained.
The clothes weren't mine, they were picked out, zipped up, approved by someone else.
The shoots weren't my choice, they were decided by my agents.
I simply showed up and played the part.
I became what I thought the world wanted me to be—desirable, valuable, enough.
I believed if I could just keep getting it right on the outside, maybe the inside would eventually feel right too.

Looking at those photos that day in my office felt bittersweet.
I remember how it felt to be her. To believe so deeply that I had to become something other than myself to be worthy.
To be chosen. To be seen.

That girl in the photos had no idea how beautiful she really was. All she could see were the parts she thought needed fixing; the stomach that wasn't flat enough, the face that wasn't symmetrical enough, the body that didn't match the sample size. She was always chasing an ideal she didn't create, one that whispered, *almost... but not quite.*

And it's wild looking at those photos now because I can see how wrong I was.

I wasn't flawed. I wasn't lacking. What I was missing wasn't captured in a photograph. It was the internal things—self-worth, safety, permission to take up space without having to earn it. I didn't know how to love myself without performing. I didn't know I didn't have to prove my value to be valuable.

I wasn't perfect in the way I thought I had to be. But I was whole. I was radiant. I just couldn't feel it. I was too busy tailoring myself to match someone else's vision. Too busy chasing a standard that was impossible to meet, one that shifted every time I got close.

I traced my fingers along the edge of a photo where I wore my hair in deep red waves. I chuckled looking at that photo. The red hair. It brought me right back to Los Angeles.

The air carried that heady combination of sweet-scented sun-baked pavement and the saccharine smell of coconut sunscreen and heavy perfume. I remember when I first landed in L.A., that scent combination felt like freedom. It eventually started to feel like pressure. Pressure to be more. To hustle. To shine brighter than the girl standing next to you.

It was the kind of place where everyone was chasing something, and no one ever really arrived.

I dyed my hair red after seeing a girl with the same shade get booked on a show I desperately wanted. She stood out. And in that world, standing out meant survival. So I booked the appointment, showed my hairdresser a photo of a beautiful redhead super model, and said, "Make me this."

And for a time, it worked.

People noticed. Not just looked, noticed.
Compliments. Callbacks. Bookings.
Redheads were rare in Los Angeles, and I had finally become something that felt valuable.

It was exciting.
Electric, even.

I was twenty years old and living the life I used to dream about as a teenager when I would flip through fashion magazines in my small town. The shoots, the castings, the wardrobe racks, the energy of it all, it felt like I was the main character in my childhood dreams..

But underneath it all,
I was disappearing.

The more I was praised for becoming what they wanted, the less I trusted who I really was.

Every choice I made or agreed to—the hair color, the outfits, the way I posed, smiled, moved—was pulling me further from myself. I wasn't living in alignment. I was constantly contorting myself just to keep up, to fit inside something—an outfit, an ideal, an expectation. I didn't question it. In fact, I thought it meant I was doing something right.

Because in that world, being wanted meant being worthy.

I flipped to the next page in my portfolio and found a glossy close-up from a hair product campaign. That photo unlocked the memory of the entire day in an instant.

I was sitting in the chair for hours while stylists adjusted every inch of me. The lighting, the contour, the lashes, the gloss. I was made to look flawless. And when they finally finished, I looked in the mirror and saw someone truly stunning.

But I didn't recognize her.

She was beautiful, yes, but it wasn't me. And right then, something subtle and dangerous settled in: A belief that without all the extras, I wasn't enough. That without the makeup, the hair, the lighting, the angles, I didn't measure up.

I remember thinking that I needed to look like this all the time.

It warped my sense of beauty. The more I was made up, the more I disappeared. The more polished I looked, the further I felt from myself. My internal messaging didn't start then, but it was solidified in L.A. My worth lived in how I appeared to others, not in who I was.

No one ever told me otherwise. No one ever said you are more than your reflection. No one taught me that your essence, your soul, your softness, your you-ness, was where your true value lived.

It was always about the outside. The angles. The image. The praise came when I got that part right. And so I kept trying. Fixing. Polishing. Shrinking. Performing.

That was the education.

And I was an eager student.

Later that day on set, I remember slipping into the bathroom and sitting on the toilet lid, holding my stomach. I was hungry, but afraid to eat. My hands trembled from so much caffeine. My skin was glowing, but my mind was cloudy and loud with doubt:

You better keep this up.
You better not screw this up.
If they like you today, they'll expect more tomorrow.

There was no joy in it.
Only pressure.
The reality was far different from the dream.

And underneath that pressure was a hushed sadness.

Because the truth was, I thought this would fix me.
That if I got the job, nailed the shoot, was chosen enough times, I would finally feel complete.

But I didn't. No matter how many times those things happened, I never felt whole—never enough, never worthy.

My dream of modeling slowly and silently chipped away at me. Every room I entered required me to become someone else. Every job rewarded me for not being myself.

Through it all, I embodied a belief I would carry deep within me, that I had to perform to belong. That who I really was might not be enough.

And deep within this belief I created a pattern, one that would show up in every chapter that followed: in careers, relationships, motherhood. One that would take decades to uncover, unravel, unbecome.

It was so difficult to dismantle the belief and the pattern because at that time in my life, it wasn't obvious. I didn't see the pattern as destructive. It was thrilling. It was L.A. It was everything I thought I wanted.

But behind every bright light, there was a personal cost. And the girl who once dreamed of seeing herself in the magazines? She was slowly being replaced by a version of herself she thought the world would love more. She didn't know she was vanishing.

But I see her now. In these photographs, in myself. And I'm calling her back. Piece by piece, breath by breath, I'm letting her return, the softness, the joy, the unedited parts of me that existed before the veneer of L.A. She doesn't need to disappear anymore.

I closed the portfolio, letting my fingers linger just a little longer on the supple leather. Not out of longing for that time in my life, but out of love of who that girl was. For the girl underneath it all, the one who tried so hard to become what the world demanded, not knowing she was already everything.

I can hold her now, gently.

Not with shame for what those years brought and offered. Not with regret for dreams unfulfilled. But with the tenderness she never knew she deserved, simply by being.

THE AFTERMATH

We landed in the coastal city just after sunset. The sky was that soft, moody grey that only the west coast can pull off. As we stepped into the salty air, I could already feel my breath deepen. The trees were taller here. Older. Wiser, maybe. The kind of trees that have weathered lifetimes and storms and still choose to grow.

I was traveling with someone I love deeply. A woman I'd known in passing for years, but who I truly found when we were both off work, shattered in our own ways, grieving similar things in silence. We worked for the same police service, but our jobs never crossed paths. We only became close when our pain aligned, when we both stripped out of our uniforms and into the truth of who we were underneath. Our connection was instant. Soul-sister kind of deep. She's seen me at my worst and has walked beside me as I pieced myself back together. This trip was sacred for both of us, not a vacation, a pilgrimage.

We had come to the coast to teach a trauma-informed puppy yoga class to a group of first responders at a treatment center. I was also speaking at a women's summit in a few days in honor of the collaborative book I contributed to, a chapter that revealed the story I mention at the beginning of this book. This trip was about healing, about truth-telling, and about walking forward without hiding anymore.

But first, we gave ourselves a few days to breathe.

Our first stop was a small town nestled right along the coast and it was everything I hoped it would be. Wide beaches that seemed to stretch into forever. Trails lined with moss and untamed silence. Mountains in the distance, ocean at our feet. For two days, we wandered. We hiked, we laughed, we cried. I felt the pull of the land and the sea, like it was holding me perfectly in place—lovingly settled in the liminal space between the two. I felt like I was allowed to just be. No explaining. No fixing. Just being a woman who had come through hell and still wanted to heal.

Of all the classes we've taught, none stays with me like the day we taught at the trauma center.

The energy walking into that room was heavy, as you'd expect. First responders don't show you their hearts right away. You could feel it, the guardedness, the tension, the internal bracing. Some looked curious. Others skeptical. Most just quiet. One man, in particular, stood out. Rigid posture, no eye contact, arms crossed so tight it looked painful. I felt him before I even spoke to him.

But then the puppies came in.

That's always the moment. The unlocking.

One by one, the animals made their way onto mats and into hearts. I saw the man's shoulders drop. A tiny flicker of a smile. I heard a woman laugh, like a real laugh, not the polite kind. The room began to soften. By the end of the class, they were talking. Telling stories. Sharing pain and glimpses of hope. That same man who came in so closed off started telling me about his own trauma. He opened up to my friend too. The whole room had transformed.

As we left, my friend grabbed my arm, looked me in the eye, and said, "Erin, what you're doing is magic."

I felt it too because I knew it. It's what saved me. I'm not fully healed but puppy yoga was what pulled me through the darkest times. It's what helped me connect to my emotions again, to my breath, to the feeling of being safe in my body. And now I get to give that to others.

We spent the next few days fully immersed in nature, wandering along forest trails lined with towering trees and thick, vibrant greenery. There was a soundlessness in the air, a quiet that settled over us like a thick morning mist—muted, still, comforting. Over the days a tranquility seeped into my bones. We weren't rushing. We weren't performing. We were simply there, in every moment of awe, in every steep step, in every breeze brushing against our skin. I felt centered, fully myself, and able to take one deep breath after the other.

The summit was next. While I was excited to connect with my fellow authors, it felt jarring to leave the sanctity of the forest and face the weight of exposing myself through the in-person sharing of my story. I was nervous. I wanted to do a good job. I wanted to sound eloquent, grounded. I wanted to offer value to every woman who showed up and paid to be there. I wanted them to feel something, but I also wanted them to believe me. To believe in me. And so, without even realizing it, I slipped back into the old Erin, the police officer, the instructor, the woman who knew how to speak about trauma without actually feeling it.

I shared my story. I talked about somatic trauma and how it lives in the body, how it manifests in illness and anxiety and the need to disconnect. I was proud of what I said, but I didn't feel it while I was saying it. I talked about some of the most painful things I've lived through like I was reading a case file about someone else.

Because in policing, that's what you do. You separate. You suppress. You perform.

I realized later maybe that's what I needed to get through my talk. Maybe you can't fall apart on stage. But I also realized that's not who I am anymore. I don't want to just tell my story. I want to live in it while I tell it, at least partially. I want to show people what healing looks like, not just talk about it like it's a theory.

The summit itself was beautiful. Woman after woman shared her truth—raw, real, brave. You could see the energy in the room settle as we all softened together. Shoulders dropped. Arms unfolded. People began to cry. There was this unspoken permission that bloomed in the space: It's okay to feel here. You're safe.

And I was proud to be part of it. To stand on that stage and share my story, even if my heart was still figuring out how to come along with me.

But I didn't prepare for what came next.

Our red-eye flight was brutal. No sleep, barely any food or water, and a three hour drive home after touching down. I walked into my house like a ghost of myself. I didn't feel grounded. I didn't feel safe. Home felt wrong. David didn't feel like comfort. I didn't feel anything, really, and that scared me. My body felt jittery, unstable, like I was floating just above the floor. It took me a full day to understand: I was still in my trauma. Still in the energy of everything I had opened by sharing my story. Still carrying the emotions and the vulnerability but without the container to hold it anymore. For years I knew how to keep it all in. It wasn't healthy, it was harming me, but I was contained. I knew how to hold it.

Except I have spent years slowly pulling apart that container, breaking down the walls. I learned through countless therapy sessions that my methods of handling my trauma were maladaptive. So when I opened myself wide at the summit I didn't have a plan in place for how to close myself again, for how to protect myself from the unearthing of my experience.

It wasn't until I had returned home and was sitting in these feelings that felt an awful lot like I did years prior that I stopped and looked at why I might be feeling this way. And what I saw was that I had been reliving my trauma for quite some time.

I'd spoken about it briefly at the trauma center. I'd spent time with those who have similar experiences to my own. I'd opened up again at the summit. And in between those moments, my friend and I, both on our own healing paths, had spent our days walking and talking and exploring, not just the forests of Vancouver Island, but the wounds inside us. We were in it. Deeply in it.

But it wasn't just this time on the West Coast. I had already been immersed in it long before I ever got on the plane. Writing this book has peeled back layers I didn't even know I still had left uncovered. Every chapter I revisit, every story I bring to the page, requires me to re-enter it, to live it again in my body before I can set it down in words. It's been both cathartic and brutal. So by the time I landed on the island, I was already raw, like my skin had been scrubbed by the hard wool of my memories. Which is why that week didn't just jostle me, it shook me; the ground beneath me wasn't steady to begin with.

When a wound is still tender, pressing on it will cause it to ache. I didn't associate how exposed and vulnerable I already felt through the writing of this book with how bringing that level of exposure and vulnerability to in-person events would put so much pressure on the wounds.

It was as if I had been opened wide in spaces that felt sacred, healing, alive—inside the forest, with people also healing from similar experiences, from the safety of the summit—and then I flew home without knowing how to hold that openness safely inside me. I could not hold all of this within me in the same ways that I have for decades.

This trip taught me that I need to build in ways to deeply care for myself. I need stillness. I need gentleness. I need to treat myself like someone who just walked through a desert and needs cool water and rest.

Because when I don't, when I rush back into life without tending to the parts of me I just exposed, I become reactive. Overwhelmed. Disoriented. And I try to stuff myself back into a container that no longer exists.

My system wasn't being dramatic, it was just raw. I had opened my heart, peeled back old layers, and stood in front of a room sharing things I had buried for decades.

And now, I know what to do next time. Not shut down. Not shame myself. But gently close what I opened. With care. With grace. With love.

TELLING
THE
BOYS

I didn't know exactly what story I was going to tell when I said yes to writing in a collaborative book, I just knew I had one.

Actually, I had many.

Like most women I know, I carried chapters inside me I hadn't written, some I hadn't even said out loud. But something about this invitation stirred something deeper. A quiet knowing that maybe it was time to tell some of those stories.

The book was a collaborative project, twelve women, twelve stories, one chapter each. One chance to speak a truth we'd carried, hidden, survived.

I had agreed to a Zoom call with one of the editors who was helping guide us through the writing process. She was lovely. Kind. But direct. I was running a few minutes late and when I finally joined the call, she said, "Okay, we have twenty minutes. I want you to tell me your entire life from birth to now. Go."

I laughed. "I'm almost fifty," I told her. "I don't think I can sum that up in twenty minutes."

She smiled. "Just give me the highlights. I'll stop you when I want to dig deeper."

So I started. I told her I was born on August 15th. That my sister was born on my birthday one year later. That my mom was diagnosed with MS when I was ten. That I moved out at seventeen. That I moved to Los Angeles at nineteen. That I was a model. That I…

"Wait," she interrupted. "You moved out at seventeen?"

"Yes," I said, "I had a falling out with my dad."

She let me continue. I told her I'd moved to L.A. with my ex-husband, and again, she stopped me. "Go back," she said. "I want to hear the story of that seventeen year old version of you. The one who left home."

And I froze.

There was no way in hell I was going to tell her that story.

At that point in my life, I had only ever said those words out loud once, in a room full of other first responder women at a retreat. With a trauma doctor beside me. It was one of the safest containers I had ever felt. There were no eyes of judgment, no fear of my words being passed on. It was a moment held in confidence and compassion.

This was different. This was someone I didn't know, asking me to unearth something I'd buried so deep, I wasn't sure I'd ever share again.

But what was I going to say, "Sorry, I can't?" I was terrified that if I refused, she might think I wasn't ready to write the chapter at all. So I took a breath, and I told her.

And she barely flinched. She just nodded, listening with steady, quiet presence. And when I finished, she simply said, "Okay, carry on."

I honestly couldn't tell you what else I said after that. I don't remember how I wrapped up my story or what other pieces I shared. All I remember is how she looked at me, calmly and clearly, and said, "I think this is the piece that's been missing. This is your opening, the place where freedom begins, if you let it."

Then she said something that altered my perspective of telling the story.

"You've told me this story is known by others, that you've lived in fear of them telling it for you. What if this is your opportunity to take that power back? What if you got to tell it first, on your own terms, in your own words?"

I was crying before she even finished speaking. I didn't even realize how scared I was until the tears came.

She had another client to speak with, so she asked me to send her a voice note later, just to check in. She wanted to make sure I was okay. And she was sincere, thoughtful, kind, trauma-aware in all the ways I needed her to be in that moment.

I couldn't sleep that night. Her words sat deep within me. My chest was tight, my thoughts racing in loops, never settling on one thing. My mind ran through every version of the future, what people would say, how they might look at me differently, how my story might ripple in ways I couldn't control.

The fear wasn't small. It wasn't just nerves or self-doubt.
It was primal.
It sat in my gut like a stone.
It pressed against my ribs and whispered lies that very much felt like truths: You'll ruin everything. They'll never see you the same. You'll lose their respect. Their love.

I wasn't just afraid of being judged.
I was afraid of being discarded.
Of being seen… and then left.

And worst of all, beyond every single one of those thoughts was: What would my sons think?

The voice that rose up inside me was the same one that had protected me for decades. *Don't do it. Don't ruin what's good. Don't shatter their image of you. Don't be the reason they carry shame.*

But alongside that voice, there was another one. This one was more grounded, steadier, older, wiser. It spoke gently as though leaning in to share something profound: You're done holding this. You're done hiding. It's time.

And that's when I decided to tell the truth. I took myself away for three days, to a secluded cottage and wrote through tears, rage, grief, shame, and eventually, release. It was messy. It was dramatic. It was an excavation. But I did it. I wrote the chapter. I took a story that I held for decades and let it now live on the page. The power it held over me was diminished. I had claimed my voice over my story.

But there were still two people who didn't know.

My sons.

They had no idea who I had been at seventeen. Of course they didn't, I had kept that part of myself locked away for over three decades.

But now it was about to be in print. And I couldn't let them find out from a book. I had to tell them.

Telling them was a whole emotional journey of its own. I didn't want either of them to carry it alone, so I waited until both were home for Christmas. It was the only time their schedules aligned.

A few days before, I asked them, jokingly, "Do you want me to ruin Christmas Eve or Christmas Day?" I laughed to keep it light, but inside I felt sick.

It was Christmas Eve, and we were all together, just the three of us. We'd settled into the living room for our tradition, appetizers and drinks by the tree, one of our favorite Christmas movies playing softly in the background.

The coffee table was overflowing, chicken wings, egg rolls, shrimp cocktail, cheese and crackers. The kind of spread that only ever shows up on Christmas Eve. The lights on the tree blinked gently, casting a soft glow across the room. The boys were already digging in, plates full, laughing between bites.

I sat there, smiling on the outside, but inside, my heart was pounding. My stomach was tight. I was trying to find the right moment, trying to summon the courage to say something I had carried in silence for so long.

And then, Oscar, in true Oscar fashion, beat me to it.

"Hey," he said, grinning as he bit into a chicken wing, "when are you going to tell us about that chapter you wrote? What were you, in the mafia or something?"

Laughter bubbled up, his, mine, Owen's. And for a second, it disarmed me. That's what Oscar has always done. He's been making light out of heavy things since he could talk. But that question? That joke? It cracked open the door I'd been terrified to walk through but knew I needed to.

I had been terrified of being seen, of being judged. But somehow, his joke made it feel just a little bit safer. My stomach flipped. This was it.

So I started talking straight at it. I couldn't bear to extend the time by talking around it. I would get too emotional and then scare them. I told them I had written about a time in my life when I was seventeen, when I made a decision I never expected anyone to find out about. I told them about my friend and I seeing the ad in the paper, "Exotic dancers wanted."

Oscar looked at me sideways, his brow furrowed in that familiar way. "What's an exotic dancer?" he asked.

"Strippers," I said.

My face flushed. I could feel a lump rising in my throat, and I swallowed hard, trying to push it down. My mouth went dry. My tongue felt heavy.

But I had to keep going. Because this was the truth and I was saying it out loud to the two people whose love I feared losing most.

I didn't give every detail, they didn't need that. And then I said it.

"One night, I was walking away from a customer and when I turned around my dad was standing there."

The words hung in the air as I paused to gage their reactions.

I looked at them, my two sons, grown now, men in their early twenties, but still, in so many ways, my little boys. But looking at them, I didn't feel like just their mother. In the telling of the story, I was seventeen again. Feeling the shame and exposure of being caught by my father. I was terrified of what they would think of me.

So much of my life had been shaped by the fear that if they knew about this part of my life they would see me differently.

The shame wasn't logical, it rarely is. But it was loud.

Piece by piece, I let it out.
Not to seek their approval.
But to offer them the truth.

The real truth, not the polished version, not the protective version. The truth of who I was, and what I survived.

They listened.
Not interrupting.
Not pulling away.

And that was when I first felt the full freedom from the guillotine of the story hanging over my head. Yes it was a release to get the words onto the page, but the true freedom came through telling the two people who I feared knowing about it the most.

They each came over and wrapped their arms around me. I was already crying. I explained the fallout. The shame. The silence. How I moved out. How their father had always known. And I asked, "Did he ever tell you?" They said no. Their faces told me this was the first time they were hearing it. I felt it in my chest, relief, disbelief, gratitude. Thank God.

I told them everything I had carried. The fear. The guilt. The pain of hiding it from them. And I told them why I was choosing to tell this story now.

I didn't want them growing up believing they had to hide parts of themselves in order to be loved. I didn't want them to think that mistakes, or what the world calls mistakes, make you unworthy. I wanted them to see that I was human. That I had struggled. And that I had survived.

Their response was simple. Loving. Gentle. They told me how sorry they were that I had held that alone for so long. That they loved me. That none of it changed how they saw me.

And just like that, the fear I'd been carrying for decades disappeared. Not because they said all the right things. But because I finally gave them the gift of knowing me. All of me.

I wanted to raise boys who were honest, free, and unashamed of who they are. But how could I do that if I wasn't willing to show them who I truly was? What if, by hiding my story, I was unknowingly teaching them to hide theirs?

My vulnerability wasn't weakness, it was the greatest gift I could have given my boys.

I didn't write that chapter in *Beautiful Chaos: Embracing the Unexpected* to tidy up my past or explain it away. I wrote it to finally make peace with myself. To offer my boys a version of their mother who isn't hiding anymore. Who's not perfect, but honest. Who's not fearless, but willing.

Telling the truth was one of the hardest things I've ever done. But it's also what set me free. And freedom, the kind that settles into every cell in your body, only comes when you stop pretending and start showing up as who you really are. I looked at my boys, their faces calm and open, and realized they saw me not just as their mom, but as a whole woman.

And they didn't pull away. They still loved me. And perhaps even more now because now they knew the whole of me.

LOOKING BACK

I never set out to write a book.
Not a full one. Not my whole story.

When I agreed to share a chapter in the collaborative book, I thought that would be it. Just one chapter. One glimpse behind the curtain. I didn't know that speaking a piece of my truth would open the door to all of it. That naming one secret would stir the others. That what started as a contribution would turn into a calling.

This book wasn't planned in the traditional sense. I didn't sit down with a tidy outline or a theme. What I had was something louder than logic, a pull from somewhere deep inside that whispered: Say it. Say all of it.

And so I did. Not with pen and paper. Not by curling up with a laptop in a cozy corner. I spoke it. In the car. On long drives, into notes on my phone, between tears and realizations. It came out the way healing does, messy, unexpected, and utterly mine.

Somehow, in the middle of all that talking, I started meeting myself in those stories. The younger version of me. The scared version. The ashamed one. The heartbroken one. The fierce one. The one who forgot how to feel safe. They were all still there, waiting for someone to hear them. To understand them. To love them.

That someone turned out to be me.

It's funny really, when I think about how I wrote this entire book from my car, on long drives between home and the studio or visits into the city to my boys. For a few years, I hated driving. I couldn't be behind the wheel without tension. After I went off work with PTSD, getting in the car wasn't just uncomfortable, it was terrifying. People didn't understand that part. I wasn't in a crash. I hadn't been injured on the road. But I had seen it. I had studied it. I had recreated every moment of what could go wrong. It was my job. And all that knowledge? It didn't keep me safe. It kept me up at night, trapped in my own body.

There was one drive I'll never forget. It was winter, and winters here don't play around. David was driving, Owen was in the backseat, and we were somewhere between here and nowhere, just icy highway stretching endlessly ahead.

I had been trained to know too much. Trained to anticipate the worst. Trained to never relax. That kind of knowing, that kind of hypervigilance, it doesn't just disappear when the uniform comes off.

Sitting in the car used to make me feel unsafe, my breath would shrink, my heart would pound, and a cold knowing would settle in that something terrible could happen, and there was nowhere to pull over and hide from it.

And yet, years later, it's that same vehicle that eventually became the safest place for me to speak. After months of trying to handwrite these stories, struggling to read my own scribbles, hunching over with aching shoulders, feeling like I was back in those mandatory policing notebooks, I remembered my editor telling me that there were no rules to writing a book. It can be done by voice notes, transcribing conversations, written in bits and pieces that are later strung together. So, I gave myself permission to do something different.

I got in the car. Alone. Opened the voice notes app on my phone, hit the record button, and I just… talked. No plan. No pressure. No judgment.

I told a story from my past like I was talking to someone sitting in the passenger seat beside me. I let my voice shake. I let it crack. I let myself be messy. I let myself feel. And I recorded it all to text. That was the beginning. Not just of this book. But of a relationship, with myself.

Let's be honest, I've never considered myself a writer.

I didn't study literature. I didn't journal every night by candlelight. I wasn't the girl with a notebook full of poems or a secret blog filled with essays. Writing always felt like something "other people" did. People who were smart. People who knew the rules. People who seemed to trust their voice in a way I never had.

I was never one of them.
But I am a storyteller. I always have been.

For a long time, I believed I wasn't the kind who could command a stage with a microphone and a spotlight. But my stories do belong there. Not for performance, but for purpose.

Because for most of my life, my stories lived in quiet places. They surfaced in late-night conversations or long drives with the few people I trusted enough to hold them. Not everyone got to hear them. Only some. The ones who didn't flinch. The ones who listened without needing me to wrap it up neatly.

That's when I felt safe enough to speak.

But now, I'm learning to let it be heard in the spaces that feel bigger, and that kind of courage has a purpose, too.

I've always loved stories. Loved listening to them, loved watching them. I used to carry shame about how much I loved TV and movies. In a culture that praises "doers" and shames those who rest, I'd tell myself I was lazy. Indulgent. Escaping. But the truth? Storytelling saved me long before I ever picked up my phone to speak my own.

TV shows, movies, and series gave me a window into emotion. Into connection. Into possibility. I watched people break and heal and come home to themselves. I learned to feel by watching others do it on screen, because in my real life, there wasn't always space, or safety, for that kind of vulnerability.

So maybe I wasn't a writer. But I was always a story girl.

That's where this book came from. Not from discipline or grammar or outlines. It came from my need to speak my truth. From the ache of decades spent hiding. From the craving to make sense of my life. To walk back through the wounds I used to outrun. To witness the girl I once was and tell her, *I see you now.*

Something beautiful happened the other day. It is almost unremarkable with its mundanity, but it altered something big inside me. I threw on my new weighted vest and laced up my shoes for my morning walk. It's something I started doing more intentionally this year, not just for fitness, but for healing. Trauma doesn't just live in the mind; it lives in the body. And to really move through it, I needed to move with it.

That day, I stepped outside and started walking. Not fast, not frantic. I kept a steady pace. I stayed present. Not setting expectations for time or distance or heart rate. I just wanted to move my body, enjoy being outdoors, and know that I was caring for myself. I was starting to get into a good rhythm, feeling my muscles get warm when a familiar feeling washed over me. It was the same feeling I get when I have a long drive ahead of me. That sense of this being my time. That solid, blissful clarity that I get to be with myself, without expectations, without responsibilities, without concerns for anything other than myself. It was the knowing that this is where the noise falls away and the truth rises up.

I hadn't expected it, but there it was. That same pull. That same excitement. And I thought, Wait. I can do this here. I don't need the car anymore. I opened my phone, hit record, and started talking.

And there I was, not just walking, but arriving. Into my voice. Into myself.

I used to think I needed the car to feel safe enough to speak. And I still see the beautiful irony in that. But now, there I was, on my own two feet, under the open sky, moving forward. Speaking my story as I walked toward whatever is next.

No walls around me. No wheels beneath me. Just breath, the ground, and truth.

That moment reminded me how far I've come. I used to be a runaway train, driving my life forward as fast and hard as I could. Now I feel like a boat with no motor, letting the current guide me, finally learning to trust where it's taking me.

Writing this book wasn't just about remembering what happened. It was about seeing it again through the lens of decades of wisdom and experience. Every story I told, whether whispered into my phone in the car or spoken aloud on a foggy morning walk, became an invitation to return to a version of myself I had long abandoned. Not to relive the pain—but to witness it.

I got to sit beside my teenage self, the one drowning in shame, and say: You didn't deserve any of that.

I got to revisit the woman who stayed too long, who gave too much, who kept proving and performing, and say: You were surviving the best way you knew how.

I got to find the mother in me, not just for my sons, but for myself. To hold my own hand. To say: It's okay now. You can rest.

There is something sacred in storytelling when it's done without the need to be right, or eloquent, or impressive. When it's done with the sole purpose of being with what was.

This book has become my mirror. A place where I could hold up each chapter of my life and finally say, I understand you now. There is no therapy, in my mind, more powerful than that.

I think everyone on a healing journey should write a book. It doesn't matter if it gets published. It doesn't matter if anyone reads it but you. That part is irrelevant. Because the act of writing, of speaking, of remembering, of putting words to what once lived in silence, isn't about creating something for others—it's about meeting yourself. It's about making space for the parts of you that have been shoved down, buried, edited out of your own narrative.

It's about saying, this happened. I lived it. And I survived. Writing gives us the gift of clarity. It connects dots we didn't even know were waiting to be connected. It lets us see how far we've come and how tenderly we can hold the people we used to be.

It's not always easy. In fact, it cracked me open in ways I didn't expect. But in those cracks, I found light. And that light became my path forward.

As I finish this chapter, I'm weeks away from turning fifty. There's something deeply poetic about that, closing this book as I cross into a new decade of my life. Not just in age, but in awareness. In truth. In peace.

I'm not the woman I was when I started writing this book.

I'm not the woman I was when I started healing.

I'm not trying to be anyone else anymore.

I don't need to move through life with urgency and speed, proving my worth at every bend. I've spent most of my life doing that, outperforming my pain, outworking my fear, outrunning my shame.

But not anymore.

Now it feels like learning to rest in the stillness, trusting that life will move forward when it's meant to.

This book has become my ritual of return.

To self. To softness. To story. To truth.

And maybe, most importantly...
To me.

CLOSING NOTE

W hen my publisher first said, "We really need to think about you being on the cover," my immediate reaction was, hell no. Absolutely not.

It was one thing to write this book, to pour out my secrets, my shame, my grief, my stories—but to put my face on the front of it? That felt like too much. Writing felt safer. Words can be shaped, softened, hidden behind pages. But a photo? On the cover of a book? That's permanent. That's exposure. That's me, staring back.

She gently explained that this book isn't just about the stories, it's about me. That a reader would want to connect with the woman behind the words, to look into my eyes before they even opened the first page. At first, I resisted. But then her reasoning began to sink in. If I was willing to bare my soul in these chapters, why was I so afraid of my own face?

What finally convinced me was realizing that if I said yes, I could choose how I showed up. I could decide what part of me I wanted to portray. I was in control of this entire shoot—the setting, the style, the way I wanted to be seen. And in that realization, something came forward for me: I could tell my story not just in words, but in an image.

I sought out a photographer whose work I deeply admired, not just for his technical skill, but because his images tell a story. He has this rare ability to capture both editorial precision and lifestyle ease, exactly what I thought I wanted.

When the images came back, I loved them. They were strong, beautiful, and striking. I thought: Yes, this is it. My publisher and I got on Zoom, sharing her screen as we scrolled through them, narrowing down to the favorites.

And then she said, "Okay, let's throw the title on and just play around a bit."

I leaned in close to my laptop, holding my breath as she typed. The letters appeared one by one across the screen, bold and unforgiving. She expanded them, dragged them across the top of my head, shifted them this way and that. Then she added my name. My name. Big. Centered. Permanent.

And that's when it all fell flat.

The photos I had adored just moments earlier seemed lifeless now. I sat in silence, not knowing what to say to her as she kept moving the title around, trying light against dark, dark against light, shifting fonts, adjusting sizes. We played with it, thinking maybe it was just the balance, maybe the words just didn't pop enough. But the truth was, it wasn't about the letters. It was me. Or rather, it wasn't me.

I didn't feel alive in those photos anymore. They felt like something I was trying to orchestrate, a mask, a performance. Beautiful, but not true, at least not anymore, or perhaps ever.

Then she said, almost gently, "Let's just try a color one."

My gut reaction was immediate: No way. I don't want color.

But she clicked anyway.

Suddenly the screen filled with a photo I hadn't given much weight to before. Me laughing, leaning back casually in a chair, caught in an unguarded moment. She typed the title again, moved it into place, expanded it across the bottom, then dragged my name to the top.

And I felt it.

Magic.

My chest swelled, my eyes stung, my throat closed with tears. It was me. Not the polished, editorial version I thought I needed. Just me. My laugh. My ease. My presence. For the first time, I felt joy leap inside me at the sight of my own face on the cover.

It was so unexpected, so overwhelming, it almost felt familiar, like I'd seen it before. A dream. A past life. Or maybe just the truest version of myself finally finding her way home.

The longer I stared, the clearer it became, I wasn't just looking at a book cover, I was looking at myself. Not who I had tried to be for so many years, not the girl who hid behind poses and performances, but the woman I have grown into. When I look at the photo on the cover, I see me. The me I am at this point in my life, with all the heartache and love and grief and joy that I've experienced in my five beautiful decades.

The writing was where I healed. But the cover carried its own transformation. The moment my face and my name settled onto the front of my book, I felt a rush I couldn't have prepared for, as if all along I had been waiting for this. To see myself, and to let the world see me too.

Because this cover isn't just an image. It's the embodiment of everything these pages hold—the vulnerability, the truth, the reclamation. It reflects not who I was pretending to be, who I thought I had to present to the world, but who I have become. And that's why I have tears whenever I look at it. Because for the first time, I can look at a professional photograph of myself and say with certainty... that's me.

ACKNOWLEDGEMENTS

Owen and Oscar: You have been the anchors and the light of my life. Every step I have taken, every hard truth I've faced, every brave choice I've made, I made with you in mind. Being your mom has been my greatest role and my deepest joy. You've given me strength when I didn't believe I had any left, and you've reminded me, again and again, that love is always worth showing up for. I love you both—deeply, endlessly, fiercely. This book carries pieces of both of you in its pages, and I hope you see yourselves in its heartbeat.

To David: Thank you for walking into my life exactly when you did, and for showing me the parts of myself that still needed to be healed. Our journey has been messy at times, but never without love. Two people struggling, brought together to heal together, that's our story, and it's a story I will always be grateful for. You've given me both companionship and reflection, and through that, I've found pieces of myself I thought were long gone.

To my Dad: Our relationship has never been simple, but it has always been shaping. Life placed us in circumstances that were painful, complicated, and often hard to carry. Yet none of this book is about blame. It is about gratitude. You are the only one left from our family of four, and I love you deeply. What we've been through has made me stronger, more resilient, and ultimately, the woman I am today.

To my niece, Eve: Being with you is like catching a glimpse of your mom again, yet you are also so uniquely and beautifully your own. You carry a piece of her that still lives in you, and being around you is both healing and a reminder of the love that endures. I love you with all my heart — more than I could ever put into words.

To my family: Thank you for being my steady foundation, my constant source of love and belonging. Through every chapter of my life, you have shown up with support, encouragement, and care. I love you more than words will ever be able to say.

To Carrie: Thank you for giving me my very first writing opportunity and for inviting me to step into my voice when it was still trembling. You helped me open a door I never thought I'd walk through, and that moment became the spark that carried me here.

To my cousin, Teresa: Your belief in me is the reason any of this exists. It was your encouragement and your suggestion to write in Carrie's collaborative book that started everything. You saw that I had a story worth telling, even when I wasn't sure myself, and your support lit the path that brought me here.

To Michelle: This book would not exist without you. Your encouragement, patience, and deep belief in my voice carried me through the darkest corners of this process. You gave me space to write in the rawest, most vulnerable ways, and you walked beside me when the words felt too heavy to hold. I will always be grateful that it was you who guided me through this, and in that journey, what blossomed was a beautiful friendship.

To Kim and Krista: You have become my chosen sisters. Both of you understand the weight of policing, the silence of stigma, and the courage it takes to step away and heal. With you, I found a space that was safe, supportive, and unconditionally real. Our bond is one born from struggle, but it has blossomed into love, laughter, and the kind of friendship that will never let go.

To my girlfriends: Thank you. Each of you has held me in ways I might never fully name. Some of you gave me courage when I was too afraid, others reminded me of laughter when I thought it was lost, and all of you showed me what it means to be seen. You are my chosen sisters, each arriving from a different season of my life, yet together, you form the fabric of who I am. No one more important than the other, equally incredible, equally irreplaceable. As Jane Fonda said, *"Women's friendships are like a renewable source of power."* That's what you are to me, power, love, belonging. I would not be who I am, or where I am, without you.

To the Muskoka Puppy Yoga community: Both in the studio and around the world, thank you. What began as a small idea grew into a movement because of your support, your joy, and your willingness to share in this experience. Every smile, every comment, every message of encouragement reminded me that we are not alone, and that joy is something we create together.

To those who sent messages of encouragement, who showed up with love in ways big and small, thank you. Every word, every gesture, every reminder that I wasn't alone has carried me here.

Photo by Samuel Engelking

ABOUT THE AUTHOR

Erin Gorrie is a Canadian author, speaker, and the founder of Muskoka Puppy Yoga. She spent years working as a police officer before being diagnosed with PTSD and stepping away from the career that had once defined her. What followed was a slow and personal unraveling—one that led her toward healing, joy, and a deeper understanding of herself.

Today, Erin speaks and writes about trauma, grief, identity, and resilience, drawing from her lived experience with loss, mental health challenges, and rediscovering joy in unlikely places. Through her work—both on the page and in the world—she offers others the permission to feel, to heal, and to move forward on their own terms.

She lives in Ontario and can often be found leading puppy yoga classes, sharing joy on social media, or speaking to audiences about what it means to live with courage and softness at the same time.

Connect at eringorrie.com or muskokapuppyyoga.com

Soul Spark
—PUBLISHING—

Ready to share your story with the world?

If something in this book made you pause—that quiet moment of *"I could tell my story too"* or you heard the whisper of *"maybe it's my turn,"* take this as your sign to begin.

At Soul Spark Publishing, we believe stories shape the way we understand ourselves and each other. Yours is no exception— and it deserves to be guided with expertise, intention, and a whole lot of heart.

Whether you're drawn to write a memoir, capture a legacy, or shape your lived experience into story-first nonfiction, we'll walk beside you every step of the way.

Our collaborative publishing journey is intentionally small, deeply personal, and grounded in one simple truth: books can change lives—starting with the author's.
If that feels like your next chapter, we'd love to help you begin.

soulsparkpublishing.com
Your story is worthy. Let's bring it to life..

www.ingramcontent.com/pod-product-compliance
Lightning Source LLC
Chambersburg PA
CBHW021219130626
46554CB00004B/1289